Embracing Crowns for Your Business

Aligning Your Business with God's Purposes Through the Crowns

By

Dr. Ron M. Horner

Embracing Crowns for Your Business

Aligning Your Business
with God's Purposes Through the Crowns

By

Dr. Ron M. Horner

LifeSpring Publishing
PO Box 5847
Pinehurst, North Carolina 28374 USA
www.RonHorner.com

Embracing Crowns for Your Business

Aligning Your Business with God's Purposes Through the Crowns

Copyright © 2025 Dr. Ron M. Horner

Scripture is taken from the New King James Version®. Copyright © 1982 by Thomas Nelson. Used with permission. All rights reserved. (Unless otherwise noted.)

Scripture quotations are taken from the Amplified® Bible (AMP), Copyright © 1954, 1958, 1962, 1964, 1965, 1987 by The Lockman Foundation.

Scriptures marked (ESV) are taken from The ESV® Bible (The Holy Bible, English Standard Version®), © 2001 by Crossway, a publishing ministry of Good News Publishers. Used by permission. All rights reserved.

Scripture marked (KJV) are taken from the King James Version of the Bible. Public Domain.

Scripture quotations marked (NLT) are taken from the Holy Bible, New Living Translation, copyright ©1996, 2004, 2015 by Tyndale House Foundation. Used by permission of Tyndale House Publishers, Carol Stream, Illinois 60188. All rights reserved.

Scriptures marked (THE MIRROR) is taken from The Mirror Study Bible by Francois du Toit. Copyright © 2021 All Rights Reserved. Used by permission of The Author.

All rights reserved. This book is protected by the copyright laws of the United States of America. This book may not be copied or reprinted for commercial gain or profit. The use of short quotations or occasional page copying for personal, or group study is permitted and encouraged. Permission will be granted upon request.

Trademarks are the property of their respective owners.

Requests for bulk sales discounts, editorial permissions, or other information should be addressed to:

LifeSpring Publishing
PO Box 5847
Pinehurst, NC 28374 USA

Additional copies available at: www.ronhorner.com

ISBN 13 TP: 978-1-953684-73-8
ISBN 13 eBook: 978-1-953684-74-5

Cover Design by Darian Horner Design
(www.darianhorner.com)
Image: 123rf.com #85093814

First Edition: July 2025

10 9 8 7 6 5 4 3 2 1 0

Printed in the United States of America

Table of Contents

Acknowledgments i
Preface iii
Chapter 1 Laying the Foundation 1
Chapter 2 Receiving Your Crown of Authority 5
Chapter 3 Factors in Business Intercession 13
Chapter 4 Crowns for the Business Team 45
Chapter 5 Basic Categories of Wickedness 49
Chapter 6 The False Crown of Deception 53
Chapter 7 The False Crown of Loathing 77
Chapter 8 The False Crown of Fear 97
Chapter 9 The False Crown of Magic 115
Chapter 10 The False Crown of Secrets 139
Chapter 11 The False Crown of Antichrist 157
Chapter 12 The False Crown of Devouring 177
Chapter 13 Gaining Freedom From False Crowns 197

Chapter 14 Superior Crowns 203

Chapter 15 Strategies of Hell Against Crowns 209

Chapter 16 Retrieving Lost Crowns 213

Chapter 17 The Crown of Communion 223

Chapter 18 Helpful Assistance 229

Chapter 19 Fruit Inspectors 235

Chapter 20 Entities & Their Crowns 241

Chapter 21 Epilogue 251

Appendix 253

Learning to Live Spirit First 255

Resources from LifeSpring 263

Description 269

About the Author 271

Other Books by Dr. Ron M. Horner 273

Acknowledgments

First and foremost, I give honor to the King of Kings, the One who crowns us with purpose, wisdom, and favor. This book would not exist without His continual presence, guidance, and the blueprints He has so generously shared. May this work bring Him glory and extend His Kingdom in the marketplace.

To **Stephanie Stanfill**, my trusted seer and spiritual companion on this journey—thank you for your unwavering discernment, your depth of insight, and your willingness to go beyond the veil to help bring clarity to Heaven's intent. Your gift has been a compass through this process, and your partnership in the Spirit has left a lasting mark on these pages.

To my wife, **Adina**—your love, strength, and quiet encouragement are woven into the very fabric of this book. Thank you for believing in me, praying for me, and walking beside me with grace. Your support has given me the room to hear, write, and build as God has directed.

To Faith Whyte, my Executive Assistant for Heaven Down Business, thank you for your contributions.

And to every reader stepping into their Kingdom assignment through business—this is for you. May you wear your crown well and lead with Heaven's heart.

———— ∞ ————

Preface

Heaven is concerned about your business. As the Creator, He has always been building and He takes great delight in seeing His sons receive a concept from Heaven, then begin the process of establishing it upon the earth.

In my earlier books, *Building Your Business from Heaven Down*, and *Building Your Business from Heaven Down 2.0*,[1] I discuss all the resources that Heaven has for us as entrepreneurs. I did not have the understanding that I now have concerning crowns and all that they encompass.

In this book, we will discuss the various components of a crown and how you can utilize them to build or expand your business. We will discuss the seven false crowns that the enemy wants to build into your life and

---

[1] Both available from RonHorner.com. LifeSpring Publishing, (2020).

business, as well as the factors you need to deal with to shut down assaults against your business.

When we understand the package of other components that comprise the various crowns, we will better understand the advantages we have as sons of God who are to become kings in the business world.

We have often heard business leaders referred to as kings, which now makes even more sense, given that kings have crowns. Kings have dominions, mantles, scepters, particular anointings, and they have resources to accomplish their duties.

This book will provide some answers, but I hope that as you move forward, you will begin to inquire of Heaven for the business the Father has entrusted to you to build on Earth. Your business is designed to solve particular problems for others. Whether you are a manufacturer of a product or the retail end of the supply chain, Heaven has crowns that will help you accomplish those ends.

No longer do we need to depend upon the sweat of our brow. Heaven wants labor without toil. Heaven wants the earth to produce for us, as Jesus' crucifixion and resurrection have remedied the curse that ensued when Adam messed up.

Recently, while journaling, I heard Heaven say to me:

Keep pressing in for the crown's revelation. More will be coming. There are specific Superior Crowns that you only know a little about. They are superior in every way to the counterfeits brought forth by hell.

Crowns are forged by obedience. Some crowns are forged by consistently obeying instructions. They are already set aside but will be tailored to the specific son as they press their way into greater depths and expressions of obedience to the Father.

Many assume they will receive a particular crown, not understanding that an act of the will can lead them to seek after other crowns. You can desire a crown, just as you can desire an office. It is in the pursuit that the present comes.

Because each crown carries specific instructions and technologies, these technologies aim to exercise the domain within the particular crown as intended effectively.

Many have thought that Heaven does some things randomly, but Heaven is not random. It is very purposeful. The protocols are guardrails for one to observe as they level the playing field for all who seek the benefits of the crown.

You have long wondered why you seek righteousness (Matthew 6:33) when you are already righteous. You are seeking an expansion of the jurisdiction of righteousness in your own life and upon the earth. Crowns, in one sense, are about jurisdiction. If one seeks to exercise more jurisdiction, they are seeking righteousness.

Heaven wants the earth to reflect the heavenly realm in every way. Because mankind does not know what they are seeking when they seek righteousness, they do not know what to do with what they receive once it manifests in their realms. For some, it was the gift of property, whether as an outright gift or a favorable deal. Some rejected it because they did not understand it was about the Kingdom's expansion.

The more jurisdiction you have, the more the Kingdom of Heaven expands upon the earth. I want the knowledge of My Glory to cover the Earth as the waters cover the sea. One spot of water, in some way, touches another. One piece of earth, in some way, touches another piece of the earth. Understand that some of the expansion of My Kingdom on Earth will be done in practical ways.

You have viewed land ownership in the wrong light. Land ownership is a tangible manifestation of the extension of the Kingdom of God on earth. Abraham operated under the authority of the Crown of Kingdom Expansion. That is why he was not concerned about the land division with Lot. He was familiar with the parameters of the crown he wore. He knew it was only a matter of seed, time, and harvest, and his position would be stronger than Lot's had ever been. When you don't have the Kingdom working for you, then you seek natural advantages, but the sons know how to subdue the earth for the Kingdom. Abraham had more than 300 men on the payroll, not including the women and children. He knew about the Kingdom's expansion.

As you have been told, the act of vocally blessing the earth is an extension and operation of your dominion upon the earth. Many have settled for an elementary understanding of these things, but I don't want you or your readers to settle for the elementary things. I want them to branch out and begin possessing the land. If you have an acre, go after 2. If you have 10 acres, go after 20. Watch what I will do as you begin enacting trades with land. Some land you will purchase will be traded for other properties that I have in mind for you. Many don't want the workload, but I have equipped my sons more than they know for the workload that they will carry.

Many talk about the wealth of the sinner being laid up for them, but they expect it will simply fall into their lap. Some may, but most require the trade of labor and energy, which you possess as a son. Don't fall for the tricks and traps of everything being entirely easy. You must press into some of these things to see them manifest. I have things for my sons to do, but they have been hesitant about pursuing them and have pushed these thoughts to the back of their minds. I'm bringing them up again. I am bringing the desire to walk in greater dominion into your life.

I want my sons to prosper.
so they can expand the Kingdom.

Crowns are part of the process, but not all of it. Don't settle for one talent when I have ten available to you. Never settle.

This crown MUST be sought. It is not merely given. Seek the Kingdom and His righteousness first, and all these things will be added to you. What things?

Housing, clothing, and provisions. The stuff you need to do things with. Because of the lack of seeking, it is never a possibility. If you are not seeing the provision, increase the seeking. All the things you need are added when you seek the Kingdom AND His righteousness.

Many have complained that I failed to fulfill that scripture for them, but that is not the case. What failed was the degree of seeking. Many did not govern the whispers. Some of the whispers were to dissuade you, while others were positive whispers to direct you. For some, I gave instruction in the form of a whisper, and they ignored it because it did not fit their image of themselves, and they refused the provision it was designed to bring. When I instruct concerning a particular vocational choice, I have more in mind than just a temporary fix for one's financial woes. I am training My sons in obedience in every aspect of life.

Some say within themselves, "That (particular job) is beneath me." They don't understand that obedience to the instruction of Heaven is never beneath you. It will elevate you if you steward the instruction and situation well. I have spoken to my sons so many times, and they did not heed. They, like Elijah, had to understand that the still, small voice is a preferred means of communication with them. It requires you to lean in to hear. I want intimacy from My sons so they can follow every instruction as Heaven gives them to build My Kingdom upon the earth to be the mighty force I have envisioned.

. . . . .

The following day as I journaled, I heard:

Other downloads are forthcoming, as I want to cover some things and restore others to My sons. Many have walked far below where they could have been or should have been because of misunderstandings within My Word and incorrect teaching. Much of what has been learned about crowns puts it off to a future event, but the future does not help the present.

Many crowns
have current applications
for the sons
and need to be implemented.

Understanding that dominion is for now, not hundreds of years from now, is crucial. In Psalm 8, you are given dominion. Jesus enforced it before his ascension, and I have not changed My mind. Because Jesus has authority, YOU have authority. Because of that imparted authority, you go and preach. You go and make disciples of ALL nations. You baptize them into the nature of the Father, Son, and Holy Spirit.

Hebrews 2:8:

> *God intended that human life should rule the planet. He subjected everything without exception to his control. Yet, looking at the human race, it does not seem that way at all. (MIRROR)*

> *Understand that because*
> *__I__ have a crown, __you__ have a crown.*

That's what it means to be coronated.

———— ∞ ————

Chapter 1
Laying the Foundation

As Heaven planned for us to have dominion on the earth and cause it to bring forth for us, to know that Heaven has every resource we will need to accomplish His will available to us. With every crown comes a mantle. This mantle

---
*With a crown comes a mantle.
When you receive a crown,
not only are you receiving a crown,
you are receiving its mantle.*

---
*The enemy is afraid of crowns,
but he's **more afraid** of the mantles.*

Our enemy does not want to give up ground to us, and as we learn about our rights as sons and understand all Jesus accomplished on our behalf, we will find ourselves in places of greater victory and dominion in our lives. Crowns are not merely an award system; they are an expression of the dominion and mantles that we, as sons, are intended to walk in throughout our lives.

---

*With crowns,
you walk in your authority;
with the mantles,
you assert your authority.*

Mantles are garments representing calling and ability. We will discuss this further later.

False Mantles

Many don't recognize that just as you can receive Godly mantles into your life, false crowns will manifest false mantles, causing you to exhibit the wrong things. Some parents may have received a false mantle of a perverted expectation of their children where the children are trophies, or glorified slaves to the parents, and they are not loved and nurtured as was the Father's plan.

---

*Just as Godly crowns
have mantles, so do false crowns
and ungodly crowns.*

We want the removal of every ungodly crown and mantle. False crowns come from the wrong tree: The Tree of the Knowledge of Good and Evil. They have Hell as their source of directives and instructions, and they are designed to fulfill the purposes of Hell and not Heaven.

When you recognize you have received a false crown, repent and request the removal of the false crown and any false mantle you may have received. Don't live under the expression of ANY false crown. It's time to step into who you truly are, not a counterfeit version your enemy has sought to impose on your life. You have a place of rest from which to begin to operate. It's time to take a seat.

With every crown also comes a dominion and a throne. What are you supposed to possess? Have you discovered your throne from which you rule from a place of rest? This book will be an adventure for you.

Other crown components will also be discussed, but let's pause now and learn about your personal Crown of Authority.

———— ∞ ————

Chapter 2
Receiving Your Crown of Authority

In this engagement with Heaven, the scene was a cosmic one.[2] They showed her the background. She could see different cosmic dimensions, and Ezekiel stood in front of what we would view as a star, a brightly lit star. He took his sword and pierced it. It was the Bright and Morning Star. As he did so, a liquid poured forth that appeared pure in its form, with gold and white elements flowing out. As it poured out, the star seemed to collapse.

Ezekiel moved up to a host of other angels that Stephanie began to see. There were millions and millions of angels. She realized that the liquid pouring

---

[2] This chapter taken from *Embracing Your Crown of Authority* by Dr. Ron M. Horner, LifeSpring Publishing (2025).

from the star was falling onto the earth and into the crowns on their heads. As the last drops of liquid from the star fell onto the Earth, they covered the entire planet. She could hear a shout that the angels had shouted as they came full force towards the earth. She could see them piercing the atmosphere as they fought in the heavens. She could see from the perspective on earth that we, the sons, with these crowns filled with oil—this light and gold—had our hands outstretched, and we were praying and speaking to the atmosphere with authority, as if the words we spoke empowered the angels.

We had just seen an illustration of how these crowns are vessels upon our heads. Supernatural outpourings go into these crowns, each unique to the individual.

Although we may have crowns with the same name, what is poured out to the individual and upon their head, filling the crown, is unique to that individual. This is a picture of the uniqueness of each crown: the outpouring and the infilling of Jesus into the crown. Just as unique as each person's relationship with the Trinity, so is the uniqueness of what is poured out to the individual.

A diversity among the crowns exists as well as a diversity of the outpouring.

If each of you carried the same anointing, there would be no use for the body. Discover what has been poured out. The discovery is in the unique intimacy with the Trinity. Jesus, who has poured himself out, is one piece of this.

What do you carry?

View this in the aspect of the crown on your head, for we know it is not in and of yourselves, but what He has given. See the perspective from the crown. These are the mysteries that are being unfolded to the sons.

Ask what the uniqueness is that you carry in your crown? Ask the Trinity—the Father, Son, and Holy Spirit, "What is the unique pouring out you have put in my crown?"

The Holy Spirit will give you a unique personalization, the Father will provide you with specific authorization, and Jesus will give you a specific organization (on how to manifest it on earth).

Ask, "How is it unique for the Kingdom?"

- Pause and ask the Trinity: "What is your unique outpouring for my crown?"
- Pause and ask the Father: "What is the unique authorization of my Crown of Authority?"
- Ask Jesus: "What is the specific organization of my Crown of Authority?"

- And ask Holy Spirit: "What is the unique personalization of my Crown of Authority?"

[If necessary, pause and pray in the spirit before and after each question. These are some of the mysteries Heaven is revealing at this time.]

The crown on top of your head is full of the liquid that has been poured out, containing the components necessary for authorization, personalization, and organization of that crown. As you live, move, and have your being in Jesus, you walk in this authorization, organization, and unique personalization. It spills out of this crown. Do you know how, when you walk with a cup of coffee, it's too full and spills over? It looks like that. This is *your* Crown of Authority.

It is because it's not our authority.
This is a picture OF authority.

The authority in *and from* this crown is *unique to each person.*

Every person walks in
a specific authority that is different
and unique from others.

Everyone has a Crown of Authority.

It is what is being poured into that crown, be it from hell or Heaven, that is unique to the individual, also.

What are you making your source to draw from?

Princes and the powers of this earth pour out a vile liquid into the Crowns of Authority of those who walk in darkness.

The reason you have a Crown of Authority from the moment of your birth is *because you are <u>from</u> and <u>out of</u> the Father*.

You are from and out of
His original creation,
uniqueness, and design.

See yourself as a baby with this little crown on your head. That's what the enemy seeks to defile—this specific Crown of Authority with Christ is placed on us at birth. We rule and reign.

The enemy seeks to defile
this specific Crown of Authority.

If the crown can be defiled,
it removes the authority of the sons.

> *Satan fears when we walk with the heavenly anointing poured into the crown's authority.*

We are part of changing the Earth, part of assisting angels, part of it all. We are kings and priests.

We can be kings and priests for the Kingdom of Heaven or the kingdom of darkness. Satan fell because he saw us in the future and was extremely upset about it. He was upset about our authority, which is more than he has.

> *We have more authority than Satan.*

Hebrews 1:5-6:

> [5] *For to which of the angels did He ever say: 'You are my son, today I have begotten you?' And again: 'I will be to him a Father, and he shall be to me a son?'*

> [6] *But when He again brings the firstborn into the world, He says: 'Let all the angels of God worship Him.'*

> *God never gave authority to angels like he has given to His sons.*

Satan did not like his job placement as the lead worshipper in Heaven. He wanted the authority the sons had. That dissatisfaction resulted in the rebellion, during which one-third of the angels fell.

What we say in the spiritual realm truly does matter, and it assists the angels in many ways. They have great strength, and they do things, but *we* carry the authority.

Revelation 3:11:

> **Remember that you call the shots, you wear the crown. My crown endorses your crown. Let nothing take your crown.** *(MIRROR) (Emphasis mine)*

For anyone who believes they are too small or have done too much wrong, *the crown came from the Father when He created us* and when we choose to be filled with the goodness of the Bright and Morning Star. The authority that He has given us, we don't ever have to worry about that again. Let's pray:

I request access to the Court of Crowns.

I request that my Crown of Authority be filled with the goodness of the Bright and Morning Star.

Isaiah 53:5:

> But he was **pierced for our rebellion (transgression)**, *crushed for our sins. He was*

beaten so we could be whole. He was whipped so we could be healed. (Emphasis mine)

He was pierced. What he did created this anointing for all of the sons.

This is your original design.

The pouring out is celestial, supernatural, and dimensional, and it's a picture of the unique authorization and filling of our crowns to walk in the authority, boldness, and execution of our sonship on this earth.

Thank You, Heaven. Thank You, Father, and thank You, Jesus. I ask that for every person that hears this message and they ask for the mystery for themselves, the uniqueness of what you have poured into their Crown of Authority, that they are empowered in their heart and their mind realizing that this lie that we've all believed that we have no authority is dismantled forever.

Thank You, Jesus, that you were poured out and overcame our transgressions so we might walk in authority as sons. Thank you.

———— ∞ ————

Chapter 3
Factors in Business Intercession

Recognizing the common enemies every business faces is essential to overcoming the onslaughts that come against our endeavors. Here is a short list of items to deal with in the Courts of Heaven on behalf of the yourself, your team, and even your clients or customers.

- Accusations
- False Verdicts
- Ungodly Bonds
- Covenants
- Corruption
- Corrupted Crowns
- LHS involvement
- Ungodly Trades
- Evil altars
- Freemasonry

Entrepreneurs should look for clues from their team concerning the accusations they face. Imagine how many accusations they face daily from family situations, work situations, friends, co-workers, and family members. Many of these accusations can be unveiled in conversations with your team. In other cases, step into the Court of Records and ask what accusations you need to get dismantled in the Courts of Heaven.

For false verdicts, think of how many false verdicts your team has to contend with. Again, the Court of Records has the information on what false verdicts are on the docket against your business. Living under false verdicts creates immense pressure on one's psyche.

What about ungodly bonds? We must also address those who impact our coworkers, spouses, and children. Placing Godly bonds of wisdom, fortitude, courage, success, hope, unity, peace, and wholeness would benefit those in your business.

Then, how many ungodly covenants are in play that are working against your business? These could be generational covenants related to your business, directly affecting senior team members, or those that involve your customers or clients.

You also need to consider the potential corruption of positions within your company. Suppose you had an employee who didn't mind not being honest and would occasionally accept a kickback from a client. Once you found out, you terminated the employee because they did not meet your standards for the team. Their behavior has tarnished the position they once held, so repentance is necessary to cleanse the position of the defilement caused by their wrong actions. You want the position to be cleansed so that it does not set a trap for the next person to fill. You will also need to address the client offering the kickback and reach an understanding of how you conduct business.

We must also consider the corruption of the crowns of those in the business. Whether the crowns have been stolen, lost, forfeited, or corrupted in some manner, our companies need them restored so that each member of our team can fully benefit from those crowns.

A further dynamic to consider is the involvement of lingering human spirits (LHSs) in the lives of individuals and their realms. What if LHSs were involved in causing the turmoil in your office this morning? Could LHSs have been on assignment to cause such a thing to occur? Or do you have LHSs who simply want to go home and are trying to get your attention?

The last item on my list to consider (but not the last possible option) is the regular, ungodly trades within businesses. In the business world, numerous opportunities for unethical practices arise. Sometimes, your suppliers may make ungodly trades that somehow seem to find their way back to you. These trades need to be canceled, and their effects neutralized.

In the following few pages, we will provide some patterns for dealing with each of these items I have listed and cover these areas more thoroughly.

As sons, Heaven is teaching us how to use our authority more effectively to accomplish things for the Kingdom of Heaven. When accomplishing business intercession and before dealing with any of the factors, follow these steps:

1. Firmly place the Crown of Kingdom Expansion on your head.
2. Take your seat on the throne of Kingdom Expansion.
3. Pause
4. Pray in the spirit.
5. Call your angels near.
6. Commission them to co-labor with the angels of your business.
7. Ask for the strategies of Heaven to be unveiled to you.
8. Begin asking for crowns to be placed on your team members.
9. For those wearing inferior crowns, repent on their behalf and request the crowns for them as directed by Heaven.
10. Request the reauthorization of those crowns in their lives.

Accusations

Since the very beginning, people have been subject to an onslaught of accusations. Some of these accusations may contain some truth, but many do not. The same thing happens to us. We experience accusations daily. The volume of accusations the business faces is hard to fathom. The following passage says it well.

2 Corinthians 2:11:

> *The agenda of **any accusation** is to **divide** and **dominate**. (MIRROR) (Emphasis mine)*

If I can get you to embrace an accusation (particularly a false one), I can begin to divide you from the truth about the situation. Once I have divided you from the truth about a matter, I have then redefined how you view that person and will begin to dominate that relationship. If you believe every accusation against your team member without seeking out the truth about that issue, that accusation will eventually dominate your perception of your team member. Accusations typically start with a whisper, which is essentially an inference of wrong by someone. You should have no tolerance for gossip in any form in your business. It can destroy relationships, damage client trust, and erode profitability.

We don't have to always agree with our team, but we need to deal with accusations on their behalf so that they can function on a more level playing field. We follow the same pattern when dealing with accusations against a team member as when dealing with accusations against ourselves, our spouse, our children, or anyone else.

The steps are:

1. Agree with the adversary quickly.
2. Confess it as a sin.
3. Repent.
4. Ask the blood of Jesus to be applied to that accusation and all the ramifications of it.

In just a few moments, you will have dismantled that accusation from having power over the other person's life. You will have done them a tremendous favor.

Court Scenario

Concerning Accusations
Against a Team Member

I request access to the realms of Heaven and the Court of Mercy on behalf of my team member.

Your Honor, I present the application regarding the allegation that my team member is __(list the accusation here)__ .

On their behalf, I agree with the adversary; I confess it as sin, I repent on their behalf, and ask that the blood of Jesus be applied to this accusation and all its ramifications.

Your Honor, I await your righteous verdict or further counsel.

> [Await the verdict or further counsel.]

> [If further counsel is warranted, follow the leading of Holy Spirit and the court until you receive a righteous verdict. Further repentance may be required. Once the verdict is granted, thank the court and exit.]

Concerning Accusations
Against a Client/Customer/Vendor

I request access to the realms of Heaven and the Court of Mercy on behalf of (client/customer/vendor) .

Your Honor, I present the accusation that _____(client/customer/vendor)_____ is a _(list the accusation here) .

On their behalf, I agree with the adversary; I confess it as sin, I repent on their behalf, and ask that the blood of Jesus be applied to this accusation and all its ramifications.

Your Honor, I await your righteous verdict or further counsel.

[Await the verdict or further counsel.]

[If further counsel is warranted, follow the leading of Holy Spirit and the court until you receive a righteous verdict. Further repentance may be required. Once the verdict is granted, thank the court and exit.]

Dealing with these accusations regularly would be beneficial to your team, clients, customers, vendors, and suppliers. Without the accusations hanging over one's head, they will be much more able to hear the Lord's voice and act righteously.

False Verdicts

Accusations *affect* behavior; false verdicts can *dictate* behavior. For example, a false verdict of "he can never do anything right" will create the behavior the false verdict espouses. Anyone can have an encounter with Heaven and experience change. It need not be a presupposed belief that if you are the boss, you must commit wicked deeds or implement wicked rules. You always want false verdicts replaced with righteous verdicts on behalf of the person the false verdict is about, because how that person behaves affects the whole unit.

Court Scenario

I request access to the Court of Appeals in Heaven on behalf of my __(team member)____. I present the false verdict of _____.

Your Honor, I repent for the sins of __(team member)____. I forgive, bless, and release them according to John 20:23.

I ask that this false verdict be overturned and replaced with a righteous verdict.

I ask for Your verdict or further counsel.

> [Await the verdict or further counsel.]

> [If further counsel is warranted, follow the leading of Holy Spirit and the court until you receive a righteous verdict. Again, more repentance may be required. Once the verdict is granted, thank the court and exit.]

Ungodly Bonds

Your business is undoubtedly affected by ungodly bonds, some of which arise from people's words, the counsels of hell, or the activities of lingering spirits on assignment against your business. As sons, we need to break these ungodly bonds and replace them with godly ones, so that your business can function more freely and righteously.

Not everyone in your business may currently have a heart for God or a passion for the things of God, but they can be a person God is using at this hour, and they can hear from Him. They will hear a lot better if the saints in the business pray more effectively for him/her rather than complain about them.

Every complaint is worship to the adversary. We don't want to empower the adversary by our complaints. Instead of complaints coming from the mouth of the sons, instead we need to be releasing righteous declarations that everyone in your business has a heart that is tender toward the Lord and sees the hand of God protecting them physically, emotionally, and spiritually and that God is granting them wisdom to position your business for great blessing. That should be our declaration over our business.

In our court work involving businesses, we will utilize a recently released authority and revelation known as the Strike Force Method. Once an ungodly bond is recognized (or a series of them), stand in your positional place as a son, take the quill of the Lord in your hand, and strike through every ungodly bond. You can strike through these bonds, eliminating them quickly. An example of a ~~strikethrough is this~~. Then, request that Heaven be invoked for the Godly bonds to be placed upon their bond registry.

The Strike Through Method for Ungodly Bonds

1. Request access to the Court of Records to see the Bond Registry.
2. Identify the ungodly bonds.
3. Stand in your place as a son.
4. If necessary, repent for anything that caused it to be placed on the Bond Registry.
5. Take the quill of the Lord in your hand.
6. Strike through every ungodly bond.
7. Begin requesting Godly bonds in the person's behalf as led by Heaven.

Court Scenario

I request access to the Court of Records on behalf of _____.

I request a listing of the ungodly bonds on every page of their Bond Registry.

As a son, in agreement with Heaven, I take the quill of the Lord and strike through every ungodly bond placed upon their life.

I request the placement of Godly bonds upon his registry on every page.

Thank you, Your Honor.

Covenants

Many times, when dealing with situations in people's lives, there seems to be little breakthrough. I have found that an ungodly covenant is often involved, usually from the person's ancestors. Someone hundreds of years ago may have entered into a covenant of death, of some flavor, that has impacted that generation and every generation since. Repentance for the implementation of that covenant must be done so that the person can be free to function and live under the blessing of a covenant of life. If anyone (or their ancestors) were involved in Freemasonry or similar organizations, they often made multi-generational covenants that entrap those living at the time, as well as every future generation.

Court Scenario

I request access to the Court of Cancellations on behalf of _____. I ask that every covenant made throughout their generations, whether on the paternal side or the maternal side, be brought forth.

Your Honor, I repent on behalf of _____ and behalf of their generations for making covenants that were out of keeping with Your will for their life and that of their family. I forgive, bless, and release all who did these things. They probably did not know what they were doing.

I ask that these covenants be voided and destroyed this day. I ask that they be burned with the fire of the Lord. I ask that every taxation resulting from these covenants be lifted from their lives, the lives of their families, and their generations.

I ask that you implement a covenant of life in their life and on behalf of them and those related to them by blood, marriage, adoption, civil, or religious covenant.

I await your righteous verdict or further counsel, Your Honor.

> [Await the verdict or further counsel.]

> [If further counsel is warranted, follow the leading of Holy Spirit and the court until you receive a righteous verdict. Once the verdict is granted, thank the court and exit.]

Corruption

Throughout history, businesses have dealt with corruption. This could be a wandering eye of a marriage partner or the wrong relationships, which can affect a team member's life or their generations. It has affected the business and all those who are part of it.

We need to repent for the company's corruption and each position within the business so that corruption does not pass to others. Corruption, to some degree, has tried to rear its ugly head in many places, but that is not a reason to excuse it. As sons, our responsibility is to repent of it and get the cleansing power of the Kingdom of Heaven working in that situation.

Have the angelic cleaning crews clean up the spiritual debris left by the corruption and root out all corruption on every level, in every position, and wherever it is found to be uprooted, burned out, and destroyed. We want to leave future generations in much better shape than we are currently in.

Court Scenario

I request access to the Court of Cancellations.

Your Honor, I stand here as a _____ (adjust as needed) in repentance for every level of corruption within my business and within our generations.

I repent for my sins, the sins of my father, mother, brothers, and sisters, co-workers, and every wicked deed performed by the men and women in our business throughout the generations.

I repent for every sin they have committed. According to John 20:23, as a son, I forgive their sins, bless them, and release them.

I ask that angels be dispatched to uncover and destroy every bit of corruption in our business. I ask that justice be done according to Your laws.

I ask for the cleansing of our business and brand from every vestige of corruption.

I request that angels be assigned to police this office and keep out those who would bring corruption to our business.

I ask that you empower every team member to resist and hate every form of corruption so that it is rooted out and this business can be righteous according to Your design, Your Honor.

I await your righteous verdict or further counsel, Your Honor.

> [Await the verdict or further counsel.]
>
> [If further counsel is warranted, follow the leading of Holy Spirit and the court until you receive a righteous verdict. Once the verdict is granted, thank the court and exit.]

Corrupted Crowns

We also know that crowns can be corrupted, so the crown of leadership upon the business owners, executive team, and the business team must also be cleansed. The same cleansing must be done for every crown among all team members.

---

*If the crown can be defiled,
it removes the authority of the sons.*

---

*Satan fears when we walk
with the heavenly anointing
poured into the crown's authority.*

Court Scenario

I request access to the Court of Crowns.

Your Honor, I stand here as a citizen of the United States (adjust as needed) in repentance for every crown that has been corrupted within our business.

I repent for our sins and those before us. I repent for every wicked deed performed by those in our generations.

I repent for those seeking to steal, destroy, or corrupt the crowns granted to us by Heaven.

I repent for greed, lust for power, adulterous behavior, graft, for every sin they have committed. As a son, according to John 20:23, I forgive their sins, bless them, and release them.

I ask that angels be dispatched to recover every lost, stolen, or forfeited crown and uncover every corruption of the crowns in these offices within our business. I ask that they destroy every bit of corruption. I ask that justice be done according to Your laws.

I ask for cleansing of every corrupted crown from every vestige of corruption.

I request the cleansing of every crown corrupted among our team.

I request the restoration of every lost crown and its components within our team.

I request that angels be assigned to police these offices and keep out those who would bring corruption in their crowns.

I ask that you empower each team member to resist and hate every form of corruption so that it is rooted out and our business can be righteous according to Your design, Your Honor. Empower us to guard the crowns that we wear.

I await your verdict or further counsel, Your Honor.

> [Await the verdict or further counsel.]

> [If further counsel is warranted, follow the leading of Holy Spirit and the court until you receive a righteous verdict. Once the verdict is granted, thank the court and exit.]

Lingering Human Spirit Involvement

It has been our experience that lingering human spirits (the spirits of those who have died but have not yet transitioned to Heaven or hell) wander the dry places. Sometimes, they find their abode with someone living. They typically prefer the family unit they came from but may return to a comfortable workplace. At times, these lingering spirits are compelled by dark forces to commit heinous deeds against others. They can affect people, offices, atmospheres, and even nations. Remember the woman in the Bible with the "spirit" of infirmity. That was not a demon, but it was a lingering human spirit forced to introduce infirmity into the woman's body so that she was constantly suffering and never able to get well.

For example, we dealt with the LHS in a young man who worked as a handyman. His father had been in the construction industry. He requested that we check his realms for any lingering human spirit and detected his father, who had died a few years prior, was present.

We helped his father transition to Heaven, and the young man sensed release. However, a few days later, he noticed he no longer had the expertise to fix things like he once did. His wife told us he no longer knew how to change a doorknob. His expertise was from his father's knowledge base, not his own.

Thankfully, he was a licensed electrical contractor, so he returned to that line of work as being a handyman was no longer an option.

What if you had the spirit of a deceased former co-worker who missed the position he or she once had? Would they be willing to give up that position and transition into Heaven? I have a friend who owns a florist. He has enormous refrigerators to keep the flowers cool in.

One week, all of his refrigerators stopped working. This was too unusual, so he called me to help inquire if LHSs were involved. We detected that a former co-worker had caused the trouble to get the owner's attention, which surely did. We helped the LHS transition into Heaven, and although the owner had to call a repair person to fix the refrigerators, he had no further unexplained mishaps with his equipment. For some LHSs, the office was a comfortable place, so it is not surprising that those who formerly worked there may decide to make their abode at the office.

Not every ministry understands this concept, but those who have followed LifeSpring are aware that we fully embrace it and regularly teach about it.

When an LHS is removed from someone's realms, that person can begin to think more clearly and, in some cases, discover who they are without the interference that an LHS can bring. That is why we want the thought processes to clear up and come into proper balance.

Registry Interference by LHSs

Sometimes, LHSs can be forced to file ungodly bonds on someone's registry. These can often be detected by their sheer vileness. Frequently, a lot of four-letter words will appear on a bond registry. That can be somewhat shocking when it's not how you usually speak.

To remove these ungodly bonds and the responsible LHSs, we will again use the Strike Force Method. First, we will use the procedure mentioned earlier to break the ungodly bonds, and then we will address the LHS that has been under assignment.

I am convinced that most LHSs under assignment from a demonic guard who is under assignment from a higher-level entity probably did not want to be coerced to do what they were doing. It is possible that some were quite willing to commit these deeds and may not have been the nicest of people when they were alive on earth in a physical body. We will address them in two ways.

For Those LHSs Forced to Participate

Court Scenario

As a son, I request access to the Court of Records.

I request that the Guest Registry be opened for _____ (name the person).

I wish to see the list of human spirits who have been forced into servitude against them.

I ask angels to gather all those human spirits and bring them here now.

Your Honor, in agreement with John 20:23, which states, 'whoever sins I remit, they are remitted to them.' I remit their sins now. I forgive, bless, and release them.

As a son, I strike their assignment and the assignment of the demonic guards and their princes. I strike every ungodly bond that has been placed against this person. I commission angels to deal with the demonic guards and their bosses according to the will of Heaven.

I request that the silver channel be opened and angels usher these human spirits into the realms of Heaven. I recommend that they call on the mercy of the Lord when they stand before him.

I request that angels be assigned to clean up all spiritual debris.

I request that the silver channel be closed now.

I request angels to place Godly bonds upon their registry according to their scroll and the will of the Father.

Thank you for your assistance and for bringing clarity to their mind.

For Those LHSs Who Participated Willingly

Court Scenario

As a son, I request access to the Court of Records.

I request that the Guest Registry be opened for _____ (name the person).

I wish to see the list of human spirits who have been in servitude against them by an act of their will.

I ask angels to gather all those human spirits and bring them here now.

Your Honor, in agreement with John 20:23, which states, "whoever sins I remit, they are remitted to them." I remit their sins now. I forgive, bless, and release them.

As a son, I strike their assignment and the assignment of the demonic guards and their princes. I strike every ungodly bond that has been placed against them.

I request that the silver channel be opened and angels usher these human spirits into the realms of Heaven. I recommend that they call on the mercy of the Lord when they stand before him.

I request that angels be assigned to clean up all spiritual debris.

I request that the silver channel be closed now.

I request angels to place Godly bonds upon their Bond Registry according to their scroll and the will of the Father.

Thank you for your assistance and for bringing clarity to their mind.

For Those LHSs Being Hosted

Not all LHSs are under assignment, and they have found a comfortable abode with someone, so that we will deal with them slightly differently.

Court Scenario

As a son, I request access to the Court of Records.

I request that the Guest Registry be opened for _____ (name the person).

I wish to see the list of human spirits currently being hosted by _____, including those hiding between realms.

I ask angels to gather all those human spirits and bring them here now.

Your Honor, in agreement with John 20:23, which states, 'whoever sins I remit, they are remitted to them.' I remit their sins now. I forgive, bless, and release them.

I request angels be assigned to clean up all spiritual debris.

I request that the silver channel be closed now.

I request angels to place Godly bonds upon _____'s Bond Registry according to his scroll and the will of the Father.

Thank you for your assistance and for bringing clarity to _____'s mind.

Ungodly Trades

Throughout the generations, many husbands have cheated on their wives, and wives have cheated on their husbands. Children have rebelled, fought, run away, gotten pregnant, and have engaged in ungodly trades to gain positions, power, prestige, riches, companionship, drugs, and more. Some even to the point of sex trafficking. The more precious the victim to the perpetrator, the more valuable the trade. Usually, blood is the currency used in making these trades, especially innocent bloodshed.

For example, someone might want more riches. They may be required to sacrifice a cat, dog, or chicken.

They make the trade by killing the animal and begin to receive more money.

Of course, they are not satisfied with a bit of money. They want more, a lot more. They go to whoever was guiding them in the process, like a witch, warlock, or satanic priest, and they advise them that the next sacrifice must be larger and more significant. They decide to kill a large dog as part of their trade. They do the deed and begin accumulating more riches, but again, they are unsatisfied and want more.

Again, they are advised that more bloodshed is needed, but this time, the victim must be human—an infant or a small child, perhaps. Again, they do the deed and have the promised riches, but they are unsatisfied with what they have now. They return to their advisor, who notifies them that this sacrifice must be more precious than any others. It must be their spouse or their mother.

They may wrestle with this for a while, but eventually agree to the terms of the trade and make the sacrifice. They are possibly haunted by their deeds, but are beginning to realize that enough is never enough. They are enslaved to this trading floor and the need for innocent bloodshed.

Sometimes, the innocent bloodshed can be satisfied by sex with a virgin female. Other times, it is much more violent. Sex trafficking has entrapped multiplied thousands of boys and girls of all ages, and sadly, some of our politicians are contributing to the problem. The influence the sex trafficking peddlers have on many politicians needs to be repented of, and the strategies of Heaven be invoked to see change come.

Too many scenarios exist to develop a simple Court Scenario, but I will present a reasonably generic one from which you can build.

Court Scenario
Concerning Victims

As a son, I request access to the Court of Trades. I request the spirit(s) of _____ be brought into this court.

I also request that the relevant cloud of witnesses be present, as well as the spirits of those evil advisors.

I also request the spirits of every victim to be brought into this court as well and be placed in a safe zone for these proceedings.

Your Honor, we present _____ to you as he is alleged to have sacrificed innocent bloodshed in making ungodly trades. I recognize this wickedness and repent of it on their behalf.

I repent for the innocent bloodshed.

I repent for the loss of wages.

I repent for the loss of properties and lands in making these ungodly trades.

I request that the evil entities that invoked these wicked trades be judged in this court today.

Those used, like the plaintiff here today, were deceived. We forgive them of every sin. We forgive, bless, and release them.

We ask that their corrupted Crown of Authority be cleansed, emptied of every vile thing, and made pure by Your hand.

On behalf of the victims, I request the restoration to the lives and bloodlines of the victims of these atrocious acts.

I ask angels to gather and bring those whose spirits have yet to transition to Heaven into this court.

We forgive you of every sin. I ask angels to open the silver channel and usher you to the presence of Jesus. I recommend you call upon His mercy when you stand before Him. Begin your destiny in Heaven.

We ask angels to cleanse the realms of these present from all wickedness.

We now close the silver channel.

Evil Altars

The erection of evil altars often occurs to create a platform for ungodly sacrifices and covenants to be settled. At these altars, people would worship the deity it was erected to and make ungodly trades to appease the god. This occurred many times in the Old Testament; the instruction to dismantle them was to destroy them. The prophets would sometimes tear them down piece by piece. Often, these are now spiritual places that have been erected, rather than actual physical altars. For their removal, repentance is required.

In the past, child sacrifice has been used to further the agendas of various political or business leaders. Bloodshed is a currency of hell that Satan convinces ungodly, misguided people to utilize to accomplish wicked things.

Court Scenario

I request access to the Court of Cancellations on behalf of my coworkers (please provide their names if possible).

I request that every evil altar be brought forward into this court along with the altar attendant(s).

Your Honor, I repent on behalf of (my co-workers) and behalf of our generations for erecting altars that were out of keeping with Your will for their life and that of our business. I forgive, bless, and release all who did these things. They may not have known what they were doing.

I ask that the evil altars be dismantled and destroyed this day. I ask that they be burned with the fire of the Lord. I ask that every taxation resulting from these evil altars be lifted from their life, from our business, and the lives of our family and our generations.

I ask that the altar of the Lord be erected in its place. I ask that you implement a covenant of life in their life and on behalf of those related to them by blood, marriage, adoption, civil, or religious covenant.

I await your righteous verdict or further counsel, Your Honor.

> [Await the verdict or further counsel.]
>
> [If further counsel is warranted, follow the leading of Holy Spirit and the court until you receive a righteous verdict. Once the verdict is granted, thank the court and exit.]

Freemasonry

Embedded in the founding of many nations is the false religion of Freemasonry. Although Freemasons deny being a religion or a secret society, they are both. They have creeds, initiation rites, and their Bible. They observe a ritual of communion. They have members and seek to indoctrinate them into their religion. They even have evangelists whose job is to spread the news of Freemasonry.

Freemasonry is a pagan religion whose endgame is the worship of Lucifer. Although that, too, is denied (at least until the upper levels of Freemasonry), their constitution and creeds outline these facts. Their gospel appears to be a message of good works on the surface. Oaths bind them to one another and the furtherance of their message and methodology. They believe their law to be superior to any other law, even the laws of the nation, and more tragically, the laws of God.

Repentance must be done for those who have engaged in this form of pagan worship. I refer to it as pagan worship with a suit. If you or anyone in your lineage has been involved in Freemasonry in any way, I have two recommendations for you to undertake immediately:

1. Read through my book *Overcoming the False Verdicts of Freemasonry: Fourth Edition*[3] and go through each court scenario,
2. Read my book and work your way through the court scenarios of *Freedom from Mithraism: Second Edition*.[4]

Everyone is impacted by Freemasonry and Mithraism (an ancient pagan religion) that has infected the church through the acts of Constantine, the former emperor.

---

[3] Available from ronhorner.com. LifeSpring Publishing (2025).
[4] LifeSpring Publishing (2021).

Often, the local lodge is used as a means of networking with other businessmen in the community. Understand that Freemasons make covenants with their brothers never to harm a fellow brother. That is why if you are not a Freemason, but you are dealing with someone who is a Freemason. They may opt to work with a fellow Freemason rather than with you.

You cannot cast out what you have in common. Deal with it in your lineage or avoid doing court work until you have dealt with it in your life and in your generations.

To provide a court scenario for Freemasonry could take up the entire volume of this book. Utilize the principles and court scenarios of my book *Overcoming the False Verdicts of Freemasonry*.

Finally

To deal with these different factors in praying for our businesses honors the Father and helps bring the will of God to pass. Using these Court Scenarios will help in the process of focused intercession, which we can achieve through the paradigm of the Courts of Heaven. I have been writing on the Courts of Heaven for over nine years. As sons, we have a greater responsibility and know-how than many others. It is time we put these principles and concepts to work for the benefit of all of us. Let's not waste another day. Let's be about our Father's business.

———— ∞ ————

Chapter 4

Crowns for the Business Team

The fact that, as business owners, we should pray for our team and guide them in the things of God. However, the onslaught against businesses (especially faith-based enterprises) over the last couple of decades has significantly impacted even the most basic concepts of operating a business. With the revelation of the crowns, we now understand that these are demonstrations of crowns that have been lost.

Recently, a client shared about her father, a successful businessman. However, political tides shifted, and those on the opposing side made accusations severe enough to cause him to lose his businesses. Although he was later found to be innocent of the allegations made against him, the damage had already been done. His Crown of Kingdom Expansion had been stolen. It is likely, in his case, because of his prominence in the nation, that Satan paraded the stolen crown for all to see.

You may not face something as severe as this gentleman did, but the possibility always exists. We must be aware of the various ways Satan will try to steal our crowns or get us to forfeit them. When he successfully does so, our authority in that area is lost and must be recovered.

If a situation similar to the gentleman spoken of before happens to you, it is critical that we not maintain ANY unforgiveness toward those used by the devil to destroy our lives and businesses.

> *To operate your business successfully, you must have some life basics settled.*

As business owners, if we have abandoned or abdicated the role of parenting to the grandparents or to the foster system, we have had our Crown of Godly Parenting stolen from us. We are missing the Crown of Nurture and other crowns related to loving our offspring. We need to regain them, or else we will operate from a state of orphanhood, which is unhealthy.

In this book, we will show you some ways to intercede for your business and its team members and unveil seven of the most impactful false crowns the enemy aims to place on your life and your team's life. You must know what to pay attention to, so your business stays intact in your walk with the Father. Where you may have lost or forfeited crowns or had them stolen from your life, we will show you how to reclaim them.

———— ∞ ————

Chapter 5
Basic Categories of Wickedness

In my book, *Embracing Your Crown of Authority*, I discussed the seven false crowns coming from the red dragon of Revelation 12:3:

> *Then, I witnessed in Heaven another significant event. I saw a large red dragon with seven heads and ten horns, with* **seven crowns on his heads***. (Emphasis mine) (NLT)*

These appear to be categories of wickedness that we deal with regularly and are the basis for many of the assaults on people and businesses. The seven false crowns are:

- The False Crown of Deception
- The False Crown of Loathing
- The False Crown of Fear
- The False Crown of Devouring
- The False Crown of Magic
- The False Crown of Secrets

- The False Crown of Antichrist

As we understand the earmarks of these false crowns, you will see how many businesses have embraced them and wear them daily. The aim of many in embracing these false crowns may not be power or prestige, but rather the result of these false crowns working against the business, which is to destroy it, and the lives involved.

For some, it is quite evident that, in their pursuit of power, they have sought false crowns that would enable a rise to prominence and/or influence. However, you can have prominence but no influence, just as you can have influence without prominence. Most seem to crave prominence and desire influence, but influence doesn't necessarily mean they have a significant impact. Often, when someone is causing harm to a business, our court work can be directed to removing their influence or impact, or both. These issues are more likely to affect the business owner more than the employees.

As intercessors, we often forget that when someone lives outside God's will, they have allowed the wrong substance to fill their Crown of Authority. Many are outside God's plan for their lives, especially if they have adopted ideals that are contrary to the welfare of those under their influence. We must remember that many are deceived and are under the influence of one or more of these false crowns.

Our responsibility is to help them find freedom and begin living under the right crowns for their lives. We must also remember that unless we love someone, we do not have the right to pray for them because we will pray incorrectly concerning them. We must operate from our spirit, not from our soul or emotional realm. The Father can give you love for those in your life so that you can pray and intercede appropriately for them.

As we unveil these false crowns, you will begin to recognize when they are at work in someone's life. That will help you have more targeted intercession on their behalf. The more specific we can be in our prayers or court work, the more impactful the results. Remember, we want to see every inferior crown replaced with a Superior Crown of Heaven. You may have times when it is no longer your responsibility to rehabilitate someone wearing false crowns. Do not be afraid to let them go. You don't have time to deal with the Delilahs, Athaliahs, or Jezebels continually. May the Father grant you the wisdom to know the who and the when.

———— ∞ ————

Chapter 6

The False Crown of Deception

The first false crown we will learn about is the Crown of Deception (aka Crown of Deceit). You will recognize that this crown operates in many people's lives. Some people you know wear this crown, but the great news is that they can be free.

The red dragon gives these false crowns to the sons, to those who should be seeking after truth. If a son does not govern the whispers of the enemy in his ears, those whispers become accusations, which become offenses and will divide that person from the truth about a person.

The Bible says in 2 Corinthians 2:11:

*The agenda of any accusation is to **divide** and **dominate**. (MIRROR) (Emphasis mine)*

Deception comes in many forms, but whispers are a primary method. If someone takes offense, they open the door to deception and wrong actions. If we refuse truth in any area, we can disqualify ourselves from truth in other areas.

This is a prized crown that the enemy loves to put on the heads of the sons. Think of it as a game. In this Crown of Deception, there is a stone of self-righteousness. All the "selves" are embedded in this inferior crown: self-righteousness, self-hatred, and self-loathing are together, along with self-idolization, self-importance, self-reliance, and self-justification, which is lethal.

The Crown of Deception appears to be a good crown, but it is not.

As sons, we must be discerning. When this crown is put upon the head of a son, the wrong master is in control. He often experiences "delusions of grandeur" and thinks he is more right than anyone else. This form of self-righteousness is wicked; it will do anything to "stay right." If you haven't already, you will be presented with people who have this inferior crown.

Only the Superior Crowns of Heaven can trump this crown, as it is a delusion of grandeur. Many will not want to relinquish this crown until they're honest with themselves and the Father.

Many prophets and prophetically oriented people wear this inferior crown. They begin to think they are infallible and are certainly not to be questioned. If they can't be challenged or their words recorded, separate from them. They often feel a false duty to straighten everyone else out.

The basis of this crown is pride.

This is a crown a narcissist wears, as well as the deeply wounded person. You will often find it on the heads of those who walk in orphanhood—not knowing their Heavenly Father.

How do we guard against this? We must walk in humility, not grandiosity.

Galatians 6:1:

> *Brethren, if a man is overtaken in any trespass, you who are spiritual* **restore such a one in a spirit of gentleness**, *considering yourself lest you also be tempted. (Emphasis mine)*

Those who wear this crown often exhibit little to no humility. The sons must walk in humility, as peace will be their umpire.

Those who wear this crown have no peace. Everyone who wears this crown *is looking for acceptance*. How many broken people have we encountered who are seeking acceptance?

> *The desire for acceptance makes people susceptible to this crown.*

Many generations bowed their knee to this dragon of pride and were given great understanding—false wisdom.

When working with someone, often, if they are wearing an inferior crown, they can't see that it needs to be removed. Self-striving is involved. Remember, all the "selves" are embodied in this crown.

A key to humility is a contrite heart. Contriteness is to show remorse. Many who follow LifeSpring have family members who wear this Crown of Deception. Repentance work is key. The Superior Crown of Love is the exchange. As a parent, be sure to place the Superior Crown of Love upon your spouse or children. Some scriptures talk about contriteness.

Psalm 34:18:

> *The Lord is near to those who have a broken heart and saves **(delivers)** such as have a contrite spirit. (Emphasis mine)*

Isaiah 57:15:

> *The high and lofty one who lives in eternity, the Holy One, says this: 'I live in the high and holy place with those whose spirits are contrite and*

humble. I restore the crushed spirit of the humble and revive the courage of those with repentant hearts.' (NLT)

And then Isaiah 66:2:

My hands have made both heaven and earth; they and everything in them are mine. I, the LORD, have spoken! 'I will bless those who have humble and contrite hearts, who tremble at my word.' (NLT)

If someone in the business already wears this false crown, you must address the pride. If they don't have the fear of the Lord operating in their life, they will gladly wear this false crown. The enemy would love to give you and those in your business these crowns.

To bring people to freedom who have found themselves wearing this crown, remember that:

- Humility on your part and the other party's part is key.
- We must let peace be our umpire, not the accolades of those around us.
- We must be willing to repent and forgive.
- We must have remorse for our improper behavior. Having a fear of the Lord in our lives makes us much more willing to do this.
- We must own our pride. Many people have pride as a significant issue. We are what we are by the Father's grace upon our lives

Identifying the False Crown of Deception

- They are self-righteous.
- All the "selves" manifest in this crown: self-righteousness, self-hatred, and self-loathing, along with self-idolization, self-importance, and self-justification.
- They are always striving.
- Nothing negative that happens is their fault
- They present themselves as good when underneath, they have evil intent.
- They often have delusions of grandeur.
- They may consider themselves prophetic.
- They think they are infallible.
- Do they have narcissistic tendencies?
- Are they prideful?
- They are deeply broken underneath.
- They have no humility.
- They have a strong desire for acceptance.
- They have no fear of God.

How Do These Characteristics Affect Businesses

When this kind of character is operating (especially in leadership), it can **deeply wound a business**, particularly one that's called to operate under Kingdom values. Let's examine each characteristic and explore how it negatively impacts a company, particularly from a spiritual and cultural perspective.

1. They are self-righteous.

Impact: Self-righteousness breeds legalism and judgment. It leaves no room for grace, correction, or growth. In business, this leads to a culture of fear—where mistakes are punished instead of used for learning. Team members won't feel safe to be vulnerable or bring honest feedback.

2. All the "selves" manifest in this crown: self-righteousness, self-hatred, self-loathing, self-idolization, self-importance, and self-justification.

Impact: This creates a fractured, ego-driven leadership style. It sends mixed signals: appearing confident on the outside but unstable or toxic on the inside. Employees often feel manipulated, unsure of which version of the leader they will get. It erodes trust, transparency, and team cohesion.

3. They are always striving.

Impact: Constant striving replaces **rest**—a key component of Kingdom business. This creates burnout, hustle culture, and anxiety. It drives the team by pressure rather than by purpose. Productivity may rise temporarily, but long-term sustainability crashes.

4. Nothing negative that happens is their fault.

Impact: This deflective behavior stifles accountability and ownership. When leaders never admit fault, they model blame-shifting. It fosters a toxic blame culture where no one feels safe taking risks or admitting when something goes wrong. Innovation dies when mistakes are demonized.

5. They present themselves as good when underneath, they have evil intent.

Impact: This is spiritual duplicity—**a counterfeit anointing.** It opens the door to deception, manipulation, and spiritual abuse. People may follow initially, but the fruit of this approach over time is disillusionment, betrayal, and emotional damage. Eventually, what is hidden will surface, and the collapse will be significant.

6. They often have delusions of grandeur.

Impact: Grandiosity without humility leads to unsound decisions, overreaching projects, or risky ventures that lack wisdom. The business may chase a "vision" that hasn't been vetted by Heaven. It inflates the leader's ego but deflates the team's morale and voice.

7. They may consider themselves prophetic.

Impact: This can be beautiful if genuine, but dangerous if distorted. If they claim prophetic insight but aren't submitted to spiritual counsel or fruit-tested revelation, they can **use "God told me" as a manipulation tool,** shutting down disagreement or accountability.

8. They think they are infallible.

Impact: A leader who sees themselves as beyond correction creates **a dictatorship, not a team.** Wisdom from others is silenced. It quenches collaboration, creative input, and spiritual checks. The business becomes rigid, brittle, and isolated.

9. Do they have narcissistic tendencies?

Impact: Narcissism fosters **exploitation, not empowerment.** People are viewed as tools for the leader's vision rather than sons and daughters with callings. This produces high turnover, emotional exhaustion, and a climate of fear and codependency.

10. Are they prideful?

Impact: Pride is the **enemy of wisdom** (Proverbs 11:2). It keeps the leader from seeking counsel, repenting, or growing. Pride repels God's presence, while humility invites favor. A prideful leader will eventually lead the business into a fall.

---

11. They are deeply broken underneath.

Impact: Untended wounds become doorways for unclean spirits—like control, fear, jealousy, or manipulation. A broken, unhealed leader will bleed on their team, even if they didn't cut them. Their pain will show up in policies, attitudes, and priorities.

---

12. They have no humility.

Impact: Without humility, there's no room for God's voice. Decisions are made from self-preservation, ego, or pressure. Relationships break down. Correction is resisted. The company becomes spiritually clogged, and the Holy Spirit is grieved.

---

13. They have a strong desire for acceptance.

Impact: People-pleasing becomes the ruler, not obedience to God. The business starts chasing trends or approval instead of the Lord's design. Pricing, branding, partnerships, and policies are often shaped more by a fear of man than by a fear of the Lord.

14. They have no fear of God.

Impact: This is the most dangerous of all. Without the fear of the Lord, the leader feels no restraint-no inner boundary of reverence, repentance, or accountability. They may misuse authority, manipulate Scripture, or use "Kingdom" language to build their empire. Business becomes a spiritual counterfeit.

Summary

When these traits are operating, the business becomes **misaligned, unsafe, and spiritually compromised.** Even if it appears successful on the outside, the fruit is tainted. It becomes a **broken cistern**—drawing water but never holding the flow of Heaven.

Removing a False Crown of Deception

1. Request entrance to the Court of Crowns.
2. Repent for embracing the Crown of Deception out of brokenness, arrogance, and pride.

3. Repent for every vestige of pride, arrogance, or brokenness in their life. Have them do the same.
4. Have them remove the false crown from your head.
5. Ask for the Crown of Humility, the Crown of Righteousness, and the Crown of Love to be placed on their heads.

Generational False Crowns

Sometimes, these false crowns will be passed from generation to generation. This is not limited to this false crown, but could be the case with any false crown. You want any false crown removed from your generational line. Remember that as the business owner, you need to look in the mirror before looking at those on your team.

Repent for those in your generational line who embraced the Crown of Deceit out of their brokenness, arrogance, and pride. Repent for any vestiges of pride, arrogance, or brokenness. Remove the inferior crown from your head and the crown on your generational line, and ask for the Crown of Humility in its place *and* a Crown of Righteousness.

Removal of a Generational False Crown

1. Repent for those in your generational line who embraced the Crown of Deceit out of their brokenness, arrogance, and pride.
2. Repent for any vestiges of pride, arrogance, or brokenness in your life.
3. Remove the crown from your head and the crown on your generational line.
4. Ask for the Crown of Humility in its place, the Crown of Love, and the Crown of Righteousness.

When you see someone experiencing delusions of grandeur, look for this crown. Only the Superior Crowns trump this crown.

Remember, humility protects from these false crowns.

As Psalm 100:3 says:

> *Know that the LORD, He is God;* ***it is He who has made us, and not we ourselves;*** *we are His people and the sheep of His pasture. (Emphasis mine)*

Personal Court Case for the Removal of the False Crown of Deception

Father, we ask to enter the realms of Heaven through Jesus. I invite the Seven Spirits of God and the angels. I ask to enter the Court of Mercy.

I request that You bring into this Court everyone in our generations, both mother and Father's side, as well as those related to us by blood, marriage, adoption, civil or religious covenants, all the way from Your hand in the Garden and all the way forward as far as it needs to go, as well as my cloud of witnesses.

I request that the accuser of the brethren be brought into this Court. Your Honor, I agree with the adversary that my generation and I have picked up this false Crown of Deception through pride, arrogance, lies, delusions of grandeur, false humility, and all the rest. I repent for every self-deception that we have accepted and traded with. I repent of self-idolization, and I repent for the times when we have been unteachable. I repent for self-promotion and self-striving instead of being led by Holy Spirit.

Father, I repent for deceiving others and for allowing this crown to rest upon their heads. I agree with the adversary that we have all been guilty of this. I repent for allowing the false mantle to fall, and for wearing it proudly.

I repent for hearing Your voice speaking to us to remove it, and instead, we agreed to hang onto it tightly. I repent for not taking the keys of the Kingdom of Heaven and closing these doors, realms, gates, and bridges.

I repent where You have allowed us to use the key of humility to close these doors forever, and instead, we rebelled. I repent for the dishonor we brought upon ourselves, others, and You, Lord, for wearing this Crown of Deception, agreeing with delusions of grandeur, and thinking of ourselves more highly than we ought to.

I repent for being distracted by this Crown of Deception and allowing its deception to bring us further and further and further away from the truth. I repent for being awestruck by the illusion of this crown.

I repent for the throne, which is the altar of worship, where we have worshipped ourselves, worshipped what we've accomplished, and even worshipped the pain in our thoughts and minds.

I ask that the angels come and take this altar, this throne, and the idols upon it, which are all of our self's. I repent for the use of this crown as well as every gray and black stone representing the self. I repent for where we have pride and present the crown, the throne, and the mantle to this court for judgment.

I ask that the angels bring every spirit associated with and assigned to this crown into the court for judgment. I now turn to our generations, and I forgive, bless, and release you for participating in this crown. I forgive them for perpetuating it through the generations and placing it upon the heads of others, and I repent for where I have placed it upon the heads of others. I ask for the blood of Jesus. I ask for the full destruction of the crown, the throne, and the mantle.

I request that the stain of this crown that was left upon the heads of the sons be removed by the blood of Jesus, and I ask that it become white as snow. I request the mantles be rent in two and torn as we bow in this court before the Just Judge of the Universe. We bow in humility. I say, 'Have mercy on us, Jesus.

I ask that You walk through the timeline in our generations. Please deliver to us Your Crown of Righteousness. I agree that we have strayed because of these false, inferior crowns. I ask that You take our hand and bring our generations back to the truth. I ask for mercy and Your righteous verdict on our behalf and those of our generations.

I ask that you please destroy and burn this inferior crown which is set on the seven-headed dragon, the dragon, its seven heads, its inferior crowns, thrones, mantles, scepters, altars, spiritual residue, essences, and debris, in Jesus' name.

I ask that the Superior Crowns of the Kingdom of Heaven be placed upon our heads, overturning the enormity of our sins.

I ask for renewed authorization for every crown restored to us and those to be restored today in Your court and *the release of every mantle, throne, scepter, altar, anointing, and Glory.*

I receive Your righteous verdict or further counsel, Your Honor.

> [If further counsel is advised, follow these instructions. Once you have received a righteous verdict, begin the following segment:]

With our righteous verdict in hand, I speak to the earth. I speak to you that every one of our generations who stepped upon you, even those related to us by blood, marriage, adoption, civil or religious covenant.

Earth, I have received a righteous verdict from the Courts of Heaven this day. I bless you to hear the word of the Lord. I bless you to swallow up the iniquity and the egregious sins of self-deception and wearing these crowns. Swallow up every word and deed that was done upon you. Swallow the innocent bloodshed, sexual sins, moving of the boundary stones, worship of ourselves, idol worship, occultic worship, theft...every sin under the sun that Jesus died for. I charge you to swallow it up and bless you to your original design. I bless you to see the governing sons and to begin blessing us. Begin pouring out your riches of abundance of truth and life.

I request the blood of Jesus to cover every place this was done upon you or in you. I speak to the frequencies of the wind to blow away the evil, to the water to drown it, and to the fire to burn it. I speak to you to return to your original design as the Lord had created you. The Earth is the Lord's, and its fullness belongs to the Lord.

I speak peace. I thank the Just Judge. I thank You, Jesus, the author and the finisher of our faith, for the Crowns of Righteousness and the Crown of Love that trump this inferior crown.

As a governing son, I pick up these Superior Crowns, place them upon our heads, and ask you to help us rule. I commission the angels to render these righteous verdicts in the spirit and the natural. I commission the angels to put this on record.

As a son, I call in the treasure lost from the north, the south, the east, and the west in every age, realm, dimension, and time to fill the capacity of this section.

Thank You, Just Judge, for honoring us and trusting us to wear these Crowns of Love and Righteousness. Thank You for helping us occupy the territory you assigned us. I don't take this lightly, and I ask for supernatural assistance and help daily to govern well as Your sons, in the name of Jesus.

I ask that all of this be done in time and out of time, and in every age, realm, and dimension, and that all of the spiritual debris, residue, and essences that were left behind by this inferior crown and the spirits that came with it be destroyed utterly. I thank You, Father, for what You did, Jesus, for giving us authority and dominion here.

Court Case for the Removal of the False Crown of Deception Off of Someone

Father, I ask to enter the realms of Heaven through Jesus on behalf of _____. I invite the Seven Spirits of God, the angels, and the accuser of the brethren. I ask to enter the Court of Mercy.

I request that You bring into this Court everyone in their generations, both their mothers' and their fathers' side, as well as those related to them by blood, marriage, adoption, civil or religious covenants, all the way from Your hand in the Garden and all the way forward as far as it needs to go, as well as their cloud of witnesses.

Your Honor, I agree with the adversary that they and their generations have picked up this false Crown of Deception through pride, arrogance, lies, delusions of grandeur, false humility, and all of the selves. I repent for every self-deception that we have accepted and traded with. I repent of self-idolization, and I repent for the times when we have been unteachable. I repent for self-promotion and self-striving instead of being led by Holy Spirit by them and their generations.

Father, I repent for where they deceived others and for allowing this crown to rest upon their heads. I agree with the adversary that they have all been guilty of this. I repent for allowing the false mantle to fall, and for wearing it proudly.

I repent for when they heard Your voice speaking to them to remove it, and instead, they agreed to hang onto it tightly. I repent for them not taking the keys of the Kingdom of Heaven and closing these doors, realms, gates, and bridges.

I repent where you've allowed them to use the key of humility to close these doors forever, and instead, they rebelled. I repent for the dishonor they brought upon themselves, others, and you, Lord, for wearing this Crown of Deception, agreeing with delusions of grandeur, and thinking of themselves more highly than they ought to.

I repent for them being distracted by this Crown of Deception and allowing its deception to lead them further and further away from the truth. I repent for being awestruck by the illusion of this crown.

I repent for the throne, which is the altar of worship, where they have worshipped themselves, worshipped what they have accomplished, and even worshipped the pain in their thoughts and minds.

I ask that the angels come and take this altar, this throne, and the idols upon it, which are all of their selfs. I repent for the use of this crown as well as every gray and black stone representing the selfs.

I repent for where they have pride and present the crown, throne, and mantle to this court for judgment.

I ask that the angels bring every spirit associated with and assigned to this crown into the court for judgment.

I now turn to their generations and forgive, bless, and release them for their participation in this crown. I forgive them for perpetuating it through the generations and placing it upon the heads of others, and I repent for where they have placed it upon the heads of others. I ask for the blood of Jesus to cover this. I ask for the full destruction of the crown, the throne, and the mantle.

I request that the stain of this crown that was left upon the heads of the sons be removed by the blood of Jesus, and I ask that it become white as snow. I request the mantles be rent in two and torn as I bow in this court before the Just Judge of the Universe. I bow in humility. I say, 'Have mercy on them, Jesus. I ask that you walk through the timeline in their generations. Please deliver to them Your Crown of Righteousness. I agree that they have strayed because of these false, inferior crowns. I ask that you take their hand and bring their generations back to the truth. I ask for mercy and Your righteous verdict on their behalf and those of their generations.

I ask that you please destroy and burn this inferior crown set on the seven-headed dragon, the dragon, its seven heads, its inferior crowns, thrones, mantles, scepters, altars, spiritual residue, essences, and debris, in Jesus' name.

I ask that the Superior Crowns of the Kingdom of Heaven be placed upon our heads, overturning the enormity of our sins.

I ask for renewed authorization for every crown restored to us and those to be restored today in Your court and the release of every mantle, throne, scepter, altar, anointing, and Glory.

I receive Your righteous verdict or further counsel, Your Honor.

> [If further counsel is advised, follow these instructions. Once you have received a righteous verdict, begin the following segment:]

With our righteous verdict in hand, I speak to the earth. I speak to you that every one of their generations who stepped upon you, even those related to them by blood, marriage, adoption, civil or religious covenant.

Earth, I have received a righteous verdict from the Courts of Heaven this day. I bless you to hear the word of the Lord. I bless you to swallow up the iniquity and the egregious sins of self-deception and wearing these crowns. Swallow up every word and deed that was done upon you. Swallow the innocent bloodshed, sexual sins, moving of the boundary stones, worship of themselves, idol worship, occultic worship, theft…every sin under the sun that Jesus died for. I charge you to swallow it up and bless you to your original design. I bless you to see the governing sons and to begin blessing them. Begin pouring out your riches of abundance of truth and life.

I request the blood of Jesus to cover every place this was done upon you or in you. I speak to the frequencies of the wind to blow away the evil, to the water to drown it, and to the fire to burn it. I speak to you to return to your original design as the Lord had created you. The Earth is the Lord's, and its fullness belongs to the Lord.

I speak peace. I thank the Just Judge. I thank You, Jesus, the author and the finisher of their faith, for the Crowns of Righteousness and the Crown of Love that trump this inferior crown.

As a governing son, I pick up these Superior Crowns, place them upon their heads, and ask you to help them rule.

I commission the angels to render these righteous verdicts in the spirit and the natural. I commission the angels to put this on record.

As a son, I call in the treasure that has been lost from the north, the south, the east, and the west in every age, realm, dimension, and time to fill the capacity of this section.

Thank you, Just Judge, for honoring them and trusting them with the responsibility of wearing these Crowns of Love and Righteousness. Thank you for helping them occupy the territory you assigned them. I don't take this lightly and ask for supernatural assistance and daily help to govern well as Your sons, in the name of Jesus.

I ask that all of this be done in time and out of time, and in every age, realm, and dimension, and that all of the spiritual debris, residue, and essences that were left behind by this inferior crown and the spirits that came with it be destroyed utterly. Thank You, Father, for what you did and for giving us authority and dominion here.

Remember that the enemy is all about providing false solutions in your life. That is why this false crown is so deceptive. You may think you have a superior revelation or that you are exempt from certain things in your life that are against scripture—that certain rules don't apply to you.

> A rejection of truth on any level
> can set you up to receive a
> false Crown of Deceit.

———— ∞ ————

Chapter 7

The False Crown of Loathing

The Crown of Loathing needs to be understood as it is a great crown of wickedness. To loathe something is to hate it intensely. It is the epitome of hatred. This crown *sits with injustice* and mandates the wickedness of injustice. This crown is the blackest of black, void of light, void of truth.

---

*Satan wears this crown
as he loathes God.*

Satan's hatred for the Father is so deep that he will do anything to hurt Him. To kill, steal, and destroy the sons deeply wounds the Father. This stems from loathing not only God but also the sons—His created ones.

Loathing has a stench to it, as does this crown. There is darkness, but an odd sense of belonging comes with this crown. To loathe something so deeply can give a sense of belonging that is false and in error.

The throne that accompanies this crown is a seat of wickedness and iniquity. Those who sit upon it sit not only in darkness in this life but in the next.

Hatred is vile. Hatred is devoid of love. This crown loathes love and anything that love brings. You will find that you may face opposition when working against this crown since you are operating out of love, and it loathes anything that is operating out of love.

Hatred consumes, and it consumes the innocent. There are aspects of loathing and hatred that consume even other dark entities. It is ferocious with a large appetite. The sons must grapple with hatred against God and man in their hearts.

Do not accept this crown or sit on its throne.

It will eat you alive and consume you.

It is utter darkness. That's why you must be careful with your heart.

> *The root of bitterness*
> *is the beginning of this crown*
> *being placed.*

The beginning of bitterness is offense, which generally starts when we do not govern the whisperings and innuendos. Let love be the ending. Desire the fruits of the Spirit.

Jesus died so that no one should wear this crown, and yet many do. With what Jesus did for us, we should never wear this crown. Some people who wear this feel accepted, but it is a false acceptance.

A significant aspect of this crown is the hatred. Many on the left politically wear this crown. They utterly loathe President Donald Trump, although they have likely never met him or tried to understand who he is and what he does. He is admittedly brash and no-nonsense, but in today's climate, America cannot afford someone without a backbone. Many with "Trump Derangement Syndrome" exhibit this false Crown of Loathing. If someone in your business feels strongly to the point of divisiveness, you will need to discuss with them that your business is not ground zero for political debates and activism in those areas. Your business accomplishes things through the Courts of Heaven.

Some businesses are divided politically and will have to exercise diligence to ensure they give no place to this crown. If you cannot have a civil conversation with someone of a different opinion, it is a sign that you are wearing this crown. You may want to check your head apparel (and I don't mean a MAGA hat) if you cannot or will not have a civil conversation. Ask yourself if you are wearing a false Crown of Loathing? Be honest with yourself.

We need to look at a few scriptures and see if we need repentance work, such as 1 John 4:20-21:

> [20] *If someone says, 'I love God,' and* **hates his brother**, *he is a liar; for he who does not love his brother whom he has seen, how can he love God whom he has not seen?* [21] *And this commandment we have from Him: that he who loves God must love his brother also. (Emphasis mine)*

1 John 3:15:

> *Whoever* **hates his brother** *is a murderer, and you know that no murderer has eternal life abiding in him. (Emphasis mine)*

Proverbs 26:28:

> *A lying tongue* **hates** *those who are crushed by it, and a flattering mouth works ruin. (Emphasis mine)*

Identifying the False Crown of Loathing

- Are they filled with hate?
- Are they not concerned with justice?
- Do they work toward injustice?
- Do they hate any expression of love that is not self-serving?
- Is their hatred devoid of love and anything that love brings?
- Do they seek the destruction of those they disagree with?
- Are they ferocious at times?
- Do they act in such a way as to destroy those they don't like?
- Do they carry a root of bitterness?
- Do they carry offense?

This list goes straight to the core of **unredeemed character operating in positions of influence**—and it paints a sobering picture. If these characteristics are present in the leadership or culture of a business, especially one that claims to embody Kingdom values, they create an environment that is not only toxic but also **spiritually dangerous.**

How Do These Characteristics Affect Businesses

Let's unpack how each of these can *negatively impact a business*, both naturally and supernaturally.

1. Are they filled with hate?

Impact: Hate is anti-love and anti-Kingdom. When hate resides in leadership—even if it's hidden under a professional veneer—it poisons every interaction. It leaks into decision-making, team dynamics, customer service, and brand culture. Hate alienates clients, erodes team morale, and grieves the Spirit of God.

2. Are they not concerned with justice?

Impact: Indifference to justice leads to exploitation—whether of people, resources, or time. A business built on Kingdom principles must uphold righteousness and fairness. If justice is neglected, corruption takes root, and the company becomes complicit in systemic harm, internally and externally.

3. Do they work toward injustice?

Impact: This moves from passivity to active harm. Working toward injustice by oppressing voices, manipulating policies, or enabling unethical practices invites the **judgment of God** (Micah 6:8). What begins as gain eventually becomes rot in the foundation.

4. Do they hate any expression of love that is not self-serving?

Impact: This reveals a narcissistic or controlling spirit. It punishes empathy, authenticity, and servant-heartedness—all core to a Kingdom business. The result is a cold, transactional environment where people are used rather than nurtured.

---

5. Is their hatred devoid of love and anything that love brings?

Impact: Where love is absent, trust cannot grow. Peace, safety, creativity, and collaboration all flow from love. Without it, a business becomes militarized, driven by performance, fear, or a desire for dominance. It becomes a machine, not a mission.

---

6. Do they seek the destruction of those they disagree with?

Impact: Vengeance and spitefulness in business are a form of **spiritual warfare in reverse.** This kind of posture opens doors to demonic interference, as it violates God's nature of mercy and reconciliation. It creates a climate of fear, retaliation, and paranoia.

---

7. Are they ferocious at times?

Impact: Ferocity, when not submitted to the Spirit, becomes a tool of **domination and intimidation.** Team members live on edge, fearing emotional outbursts or punishment. Over time, innovation dies because no one feels safe enough to think freely or speak honestly.

---

8. Do they act in such a way as to destroy those they don't like totally?

Impact: This is the heart of a *Jezebel* or *Absalom* spirit—seeking to eliminate competition or perceived threats through sabotage, slander, or manipulation. It creates a **culture of war, not peace.** Relationships are weaponized, and trust is systematically dismantled.

---

9. Do they carry a root of bitterness?

Impact: Bitterness defiles many (Hebrews 12:15). It distorts perception, fuels offense, and stunts maturity. A bitter leader will interpret feedback as an attack, the success of others as a threat, and opportunities as risks. It invites a "toxic lens" over every business decision.

---

10. Do they carry offense?

Impact: Offense hardens the heart and cuts off the flow of revelation, wisdom, and grace. Offended leaders will make defensive decisions, push away wise counsel, and punish those who unknowingly touch old wounds. It becomes a barrier between Heaven and the boardroom.

Final Thoughts:

When hatred, bitterness, and offense are in the driver's seat, the business becomes spiritually unsafe. It transitions from a Kingdom enterprise to a **carnal empire.** Heaven's favor lifts, and the company may continue to operate—but now in its own strength, bearing the weight of demonic consequences.

This kind of business needs **deliverance, repentance, and realignment.** Healing must come not just to individuals but to the culture itself.

Removal of the Crown of Loathing

Do a self-check first.

1. Repent for where we have embraced the Crown of Loathing out of hatred and the root of bitterness.
2. Repent for embracing offense.
3. Repent for every vestige of hatred, disrespect, dishonor, and lying in your own life.
4. Remove the false crown from your head.
5. Request a cleansing of your realms from the vestiges of this false crown.

6. Ask for the Crown of Love for yourself.
7. Pray in the spirit for yourself.

Interceding for Those in the Business

1. Repent for where the person(s) has embraced the Crown of Loathing out of hatred and the root of bitterness.
2. Repent for them embracing offense.
3. Repent for every vestige of hatred, disrespect, dishonor, and lying in their life.
4. Remove the false crown from their head.
5. Request a cleansing of their realms from the vestiges of this false crown.
6. Ask for the Crown of Love to be placed upon them.
7. Pray in the spirit for them.

Personal Court Case
for the Removal of the Crown of Loathing

Father, I ask to step into the Court of Mercy to receive mercy in our time of need. I request the accuser of the brethren be brought in as well as our generations, those related to us by blood, marriage, adoption, civil or religious covenant, all the way from Your hand in the garden and sd as far forward as it needs to go, as well as my cloud of witnesses.

I come to you, and I repent for embracing the Crown of Loathing out of hatred and the root of bitterness. I repent for embracing offense, and I repent for every vestige of hatred, disrespect, dishonor, and lying in our own lives.

I repent where I have ever loathed anyone or anything in our generations, I repent where I have allowed, agreed with, or perpetuated the spirit of antichrist, but also were those who are or were anti-God, where we allowed this inferior crown to bring an atheistic mentality. I repent for cooperation with that. I repent for our hatred of the Father and those who are His. I repent for engaging in the stench of these sins. I repent for sitting in league with injustice, promoting injustice, and being unjust. I repent for mandating the wickedness of injustice.

I repent for being void of truth. I repent for agreeing with, being a part of, and loving the sense of belonging by wearing this inferior crown. I repent for sitting on the throne of loathing with its seat of wickedness and iniquity. I repent for the great error of wearing this crown. I repent for believing the false acceptance, the pride, and the belief that I do not have to love you or anyone else, only ourselves. Please forgive us. I repent for loathing love. I repent for not accepting your love and for not loving others or even ourselves.

Father, forgive us and our generations, those who were atheists, those who loathed the Word of God, the truth around it, and those who had bitterness in their hearts; I repent. I repent for the utter hatred of anything that presented itself from you or from others that were or carried the embodiment of Your love or what it would bring. I repent for having an appetite for loathing and for hating you, God and man.

I ask for the angels to go through time, on behalf of ourselves and our generations, to remove the crowns of loathing and destroy them.

I ask the angels to remove the Crowns of Loathing placed upon our team's heads, of those who don't trust or believe, for it came from an iniquitous generation. I ask that the throne be destroyed, the seat of wickedness be destroyed, and iniquity be forever vanquished, banished, and removed forevermore from us and our generations. I repent for being a part of consuming the innocent and taking innocence away from others because of wearing this inferior crown. I repent for being a part of others losing their Superior Crowns, where I removed them, or where their crowns became lost.

Jesus, I ask for your blood to cover us and for those crowns to be removed from our co-workers, children, grandchildren, our mothers, our fathers, our sisters, our brothers, our friends, and our neighbors. I speak that it must bow to the Superior Crown of King Jesus and the crowns I wear—The Crown of Sonship and the Crown of Love, in Jesus' name.

Righteous Judge, I ask for your verdict or further counsel.

[If further counsel is advised, follow these instructions. Once you have received a righteous verdict, begin the following segment:]

I speak to the earth that every one of our generations who stepped upon you, even those related to us by blood, marriage, adoption, civil or religious covenant.

Earth, I have received a righteous verdict from the Courts of Heaven this day. I bless you to hear the word of the Lord. I bless you to swallow up the iniquity and the egregious sins of self-deception and wearing these inferior crowns. Swallow up every word and deed that was done upon you. Swallow the innocent bloodshed, sexual sins, moving of the boundary stones, worship of ourselves, idol worship, occultic worship, theft...every sin under the sun that Jesus died for. I charge you to swallow it up and bless you to your original design. I bless you to see the governing sons and to begin blessing us. Begin pouring out your riches of abundance of truth and life.

I request the blood of Jesus to cover every place this was done upon you or in you. I speak to the frequencies of the wind to blow away the evil, to the water to drown it, and to the fire to burn it. I speak to you to return to your original design as the Lord had created you. The Earth is the Lord's, and its fullness belongs to the Lord.

I speak peace. I thank the Just Judge. I thank You, Jesus, the author and the finisher of our faith, for the Crowns of

Righteousness and the Crown of Love that trump this inferior crown.

As a governing son, I pick up these Superior Crowns, place them upon our heads, and ask you to help us rule. I commission the angels to render these righteous verdicts in the spirit and the natural. I commission the angels to put this on record.

Thank you, Just Judge, for honoring us and trusting us with the responsibility of wearing these Crowns of Love and Righteousness. Thank you for helping us occupy the territory you assigned us. I don't take this lightly and ask for supernatural assistance and help daily to govern well as Your sons, in the name of Jesus.

As a son, I call in the treasure that has been lost from the north, the south, the east, and the west in every age, realm, dimension, and time to fill the capacity of this section.

Thank you, Just Judge, for honoring us and trusting us with the responsibility of wearing these Crowns of Love and Righteousness. Thank you for helping us occupy the territory you assigned us. I don't take this lightly and I ask for supernatural assistance and help daily to govern well as Your sons, in the name of Jesus.

I ask that all of this be done in time and out of time, and in every age, realm, and dimension, and that all of the spiritual debris, residue, and essences that were left behind by this inferior crown and the spirits that came with it be destroyed utterly. I thank You, Father, for what you did, Jesus, for giving us authority and dominion here.

Court Case for the Removal of the Crown of Loathing Off of Someone

Father, I ask to step into the Court of Mercy to receive mercy in our time of need. I am stepping in on behalf of _____.

I request the accuser of the brethren of this person be brought in as well as their generations, those related to them by blood, marriage, adoption, civil or religious covenant, all the way from Your hand in the garden and all the way forward as far as it needs to go, as well as their cloud of witnesses.

I come to you, and I repent for their embrace of the Crown of Loathing out of hatred and the root of bitterness. I repent on their behalf for embracing offense, and I repent for every vestige of hatred, disrespect, dishonor, and lying in their life.

I repent for where they have ever loathed anyone or anything in their generations. I repent where they have allowed, agreed with, or perpetuated the loathing and hatred, but also where those who are or were anti-God, where I let this inferior crown bring a hateful mentality. I repent for cooperating with that.

I repent for our hatred of the Father and those who are His. I repent for engaging in the stench of these sins. I repent for sitting in league with injustice, promoting injustice, and being unjust. I repent for mandating the wickedness of injustice.

I repent for them and their generations who hated those of other races or classes.

I repent for being void of truth. I repent for agreeing with, being a part of, and loving the sense of belonging by wearing this inferior crown.

I repent for sitting on the throne of loathing with its seat of wickedness and iniquity. I repent for the great error of wearing this crown. I repent for believing the false acceptance, the pride, and the belief that I do not have to love you or anyone else, only ourselves. Please forgive us. I repent for loathing love. I repent for not accepting your love and for not loving others or even ourselves.

Father, forgive them and their generations, those who were haters, those who loathed the Word of God, the truth around it, and those who had bitterness in their hearts; I repent.

I repent for their utter hatred of anything that presented itself from you or from others that were or carried the embodiment of Your love or what it would bring. I repent for them having an appetite for loathing and for hating you, God and man.

I ask for the angels to go through time, on behalf of them and their generations, to remove the crowns of loathing and destroy them.

I ask the angels to remove the Crowns of Loathing placed upon their co-workers' heads, of those who don't trust or believe, for it came from an iniquitous generation. I ask that the throne be destroyed, the seat of wickedness be destroyed, and iniquity be forever vanquished, banished, and removed forevermore from them and their generations.

I repent for where they or their generations were a part of consuming the innocent and taking innocence away from others because of wearing this inferior crown. I repent for their being a part of others losing their Superior Crowns, where I removed them, or where their crowns became lost.

Jesus, I ask for your blood to cover them and for those crowns to be removed from their children, their grandchildren, their mothers, their fathers, their sisters, their brothers, their friends, and their neighbors.

I speak that this inferior Crown of Loathing must bow to the Superior Crown of King Jesus and the crowns I wear—The Crown of Sonship and the Crown of Love, in Jesus' name.

Righteous Judge, I ask for your verdict or further counsel.

[If further counsel is advised, follow these instructions. Once you have received a righteous verdict, begin the following segment:]

I speak to the earth that every one of their generations who stepped upon you, even those related to them by blood, marriage, adoption, civil or religious covenant.

Earth, I have received a righteous verdict from the Courts of Heaven this day. I bless you to hear the word of the Lord. I bless you to swallow up the iniquity and the egregious sins of self-deception and wearing these inferior crowns. Swallow up every word and deed that was done upon you. Swallow the innocent bloodshed, sexual sins, moving of the boundary stones, worship of ourselves, idol worship, occultic worship, theft...every sin under the sun that Jesus died for. I charge you to swallow it up and bless you to your original design. I bless you to see the governing sons and to begin blessing us. Begin pouring out your riches of abundance of truth and life.

I request the blood of Jesus to cover every place this was done upon you or in you. I speak to the frequencies of the wind to blow away the evil, to the water to drown it, and to the fire to burn it. I speak to you to return to your original design as the Lord had created you. The Earth is the Lord's, and its fullness belongs to the Lord.

I speak peace. I thank the Just Judge. I thank You, Jesus, the author and the finisher of our faith, for the Crowns of

Righteousness and the Crown of Love that trump this inferior crown.

As a governing son, I pick up these Superior Crowns, place them upon our heads, and ask you to help us rule. I commission the angels to render these righteous verdicts in the spirit and the natural. I commission the angels to put this on record.

Thank you, Just Judge, for honoring us and trusting us with the responsibility of wearing these Crowns of Love and Righteousness. Thank you for helping us occupy the territory you assigned us. I don't take this lightly and ask for supernatural assistance and help daily for them to govern as Your sons, in the name of Jesus.

As a son, I call in the treasure that has been lost from the north, the south, the east, and the west in every age, realm, dimension, and time to fill the capacity of this section.

Thank you, Just Judge, for honoring us and trusting us and them with the responsibility of wearing these Crowns of Love and Righteousness. Thank you for helping us all to occupy the territory you assigned us. I don't take this lightly and I ask for supernatural assistance and help daily to govern well as Your sons, in the name of Jesus.

I ask that all of this be done in time and out of time, in every age, realm, and dimension, and that all the spiritual debris, residue, and essences left behind by this inferior crown and the spirits that accompanied it be utterly destroyed. I thank You, Father, for what you did, Jesus, for giving us authority and dominion here.

--- ∞ ---

Chapter 8
The False Crown of Fear

This crown operates quite strongly in both believers and unbelievers alike. It is the Crown of Fear.

When this crown is placed on someone's head, many demonic entities come with it and are released into the person's life. Picture how they may come in from a back door. It is a release of the essence of each of them because with fear comes a lot of other negative things.

When this Crown of Fear is placed upon a person, it will open up a throne, and all these negative things will begin pouring out, encircling their head and trying to manifest around, in, and through their mind.

2 Timothy 1:7:

> *For God has not given us a spirit of **fear**, but of power and of love and of a sound mind. (Emphasis mine)*

The Apostle Paul said, "I have not given you a spirit of fear," which is a specific dark entity. However, with the spirit of fear comes the Crown of Fear, and the enemy distributes this crown to many. Wearing this crown distorts the mind and even affects the heart. This crown rules over many of the other inferior crowns, making it superior to them.

Many people have this crown thrust upon them through traumas. When you have trouble receiving from Heaven, there may be fear coming from the generations. You may have to remove the Crown of Fear from your head continually.

This Crown of Fear is a master manipulator. It creates a stronghold, and when this crown is put on the heads of the sons, it is as if it tries to become embedded in them. It doesn't just sit on the head; it digs into the person's head, piercing it as if the crown were inverted.

Of course, we don't want anything to do with this crown and its ability to distort our ability to receive and flow in revelation. As a governing son, that should make you mad.

When you see it operating in the lives of others, it should anger you as well. It is encroaching on their minds. Many people are driven by fear.

Identifying the False Crown of Fear

- Are they consumed with fear?
- Do they live in terror?
- Do they always circle back to something to fear?
- Do they have a negative mindset?
- Do they exhibit distorted thinking?
- Is their physical heart having issues?
- Do they have trouble receiving from Heaven?
- Do they have trouble receiving or flowing in revelation?

How Do These Characteristics Affect Businesses

This set of characteristics paints a picture of a deeply anxious or spiritually blocked leader or organizational culture. When **fear and distortion** dominate a business, especially one with a Kingdom mandate, the ripple effects can be massive. Let's walk through each trait and examine how it can negatively impact a business, **both spiritually and practically.**

1. Are they consumed with fear?

Impact: Fear becomes the filter through which every decision is made. Instead of bold, Spirit-led moves, leaders second-guess everything. Fear paralyzes growth, delays assignments, and shrinks vision. It also breeds **micromanagement** and control, stifling the team's freedom and the Holy Spirit's breath.

2. Do they live in terror?

Impact: Terror is fear turned inward and amplified—it becomes torment. A leader in terror makes reactive, unstable decisions. Staff members pick up on this instability and begin operating from fear themselves. It turns the business into a survival environment instead of a creative, thriving one.

3. Do they always circle back to something to fear?

Impact: This reveals a stronghold—a demonic loop of anxiety. When a business leader is caught in this cycle, there's no actual progress because every breakthrough is followed by a relapse into doubt. The spiritual atmosphere becomes **cluttered**, hindering clarity and forward movement.

4. Do they have a negative mindset?

Impact: Negativity shapes culture. A pessimistic leader creates a glass-half-empty environment. Opportunities are missed. Team morale drops. People feel undervalued or afraid to try. Negative leadership often produces either *paralyzed teams* or *cynical clones* who mimic the same mindset.

5. Do they exhibit distorted thinking?

Impact: Distorted thinking twists truth and clouds perception. It may show up as paranoia, defensiveness, or misjudging motives. A leader like this cannot see situations clearly and often misreads people or opportunities. The result? Poor hires, fractured relationships, and missed divine timing.

6. Is their physical heart having issues?

Impact: The heart is often a **spiritual barometer.** Physical heart issues can reflect emotional and spiritual blockages, especially in areas of love, grief, or trust. A leader with heart issues may unconsciously lead from a place of woundedness or limitation, reducing their stamina, joy, and ability to hold a vision. It also suggests that their ability to bear **the Kingdom's burden** is compromised.

7. Do they have trouble receiving from Heaven?

Impact: When revelation is blocked, a business begins to operate on **logic rather than leading.** Without Heaven's input, decisions lack power and prophetic edge. The company becomes overly reliant on trends, analytics, or outside consultants, rather than God's blueprint. This leads to spiritual dryness and strategic misalignment.

---

8. Do they have trouble receiving or flowing in revelation?

Impact: Revelation is how God breathes fresh life into a business. Without it, the organization becomes **stale, repetitive, and reactive.** Innovation dries up. Prophetic insight into markets, products, partnerships, and people is absent. Teams start "spinning their wheels," and leaders feel stuck or frustrated.

Final Thoughts:

A fear-filled, spiritually blocked leader creates a **spiritually sterile environment**. Heaven's rivers can't flow, revelation is stifled, and the culture becomes burdened by anxiety, suspicion, and confusion. While fear feels personal, its consequences are corporate, affecting the atmosphere, the fruit, and the future of the business.

Personal Court Case for the Removal of the Crown of Fear

Father, I ask to step into Your Court of Mercy to receive mercy in our time of need. I ask that our generations be brought into this Court and those related to us by blood, marriage, adoption, civil or religious covenant, from Your hand in the garden and as far forward as far as it needs to go, as well as my cloud of witnesses.

Father, I present to you, ourselves and our generations, and every one of us who ever wore this inferior crown, who willingly took this Crown of Fear, who even distributed it to other people in our family and our generations, and even those outside of our generations where we instilled fear, we presented fear, where we were a part of fear, where we perpetuated fear throughout the generational line, or we've accepted it, bent our knee to it, or even relished in, or relished in it in others. Forgive us, Lord; we repent. I ask for the blood of Jesus to be applied to this.

I am requesting that this inferior crown be removed from me and our generational line, as it pierced our heads. As the angels remove this crown, even though it is not easily taken off, along with every binding and every structure that would keep it upon the heads of the sons, that crown be taken off and destroyed.

I ask that the Superior Crown of Love be placed upon our heads to heal any woundedness and begin to mend our minds and the places of woundedness.

I ask that the technology of the Crowns of Sonship that we wear and the new day would infiltrate and destroy the technology of the Crown of Fear and that the nanotechnology of Jesus—of His love (for He has not given us the spirit of fear, but of power) and that the power and the dominion of the Superior Crown crush and destroy the inferior Crown of Fear.

Father has not given us the spirit of fear but of love. That love is the Supreme Crown over this inferior crown, and as the Crown of a Sound Mind is placed upon our heads, that it heals every wound of the mind and that the poison that came with that inferior Crown of Fear be drawn up out of us as we are made new.

I commission the angels to clean up the spiritual debris, residue, and essences that the spirit of fear has left behind, and we receive the Crown of Superiority from Jesus, the Crown of Love, the Crown of Power, the dominion over this, and the Crown of a Sound Mind. Thank you, Lord.

I come out of agreement with every superiority of this inferior crown. I am not in agreement with it. Where we and our generations agreed and where we were lied to, and we believed that there was nothing we could do because we were so gripped by fear; that is a lie. I come out of agreement with the lie of this inferior Crown of

Fear. I ask for the cancellation and annulment of these lies.

I commission the angels to capture every demonic spirit that came with the spirit of fear that came through the back door of this as it opened the door to other spirits.

I commission the angels to gather up these spirits and take them to be judged—those that infiltrated the mind and the heart and brought the lies and instilled fear.

Father, I ask in the Courts of Heaven that these inferior spirits be judged on behalf of the sons. I receive Your righteous verdicts on behalf of us and our generations. I ask that these inferior crowns be destroyed. Thank you for the Crown of a New Day—of your new for us. Thank you for the Superior Crown of the mind of Christ and the Crown of Love. Thank You, Jesus. I ask Father for the healing balm for the wounds. When this inferior Crown of Fear is placed on people's heads, it creates ugly wounds.

Further, I request that the name and blood of Jesus destroy this throne, mantle, and crown.

I come out of agreement with the master of this crown. Forgive us where we traded and agreed with it.

I ask that you please destroy and burn this inferior crown set on the seven-headed dragon, the dragon, its seven heads, its inferior crowns, thrones, mantles, scepters, altars, spiritual residue, essences, and debris, in Jesus' name.

I ask that the Superior Crowns of the Kingdom of Heaven be placed upon our heads, overturning the enormity of our sins.

I ask for renewed authorization for every crown restored to us and those to be restored today in Your court and the release of every mantle, throne, scepter, altar, anointing, and Glory.

Your Honor, we respectfully request your righteous verdict or further counsel.

> [If further counsel is advised, follow these instructions. Once you have received a righteous verdict, begin the following segment:]

I speak to the earth that every one of our generations who stepped upon you, even those related to us by blood, marriage, adoption, civil or religious covenant.

Earth, I have received a righteous verdict from the Courts of Heaven this day. I bless you to hear the word of the Lord. I bless you to swallow up the iniquity and the egregious sins of self-deception and wearing these inferior crowns. Swallow up every word and deed that was done upon you. Swallow the innocent bloodshed, sexual sins, moving of the boundary stones, worship of ourselves, idol worship, occultic worship, theft...every sin under the sun that Jesus died for. I charge you to swallow it up and bless you to your original design. I bless you to see the governing sons and to begin blessing us. Begin pouring out your riches of abundance of truth and life.

I request the blood of Jesus to cover every place this was done upon you or in you. I speak to the frequencies of the wind to blow away the evil, to the water to drown it, and to the fire to burn it. I speak to you to return to your original design as the Lord had created you. The Earth is the Lord's, and its fullness belongs to the Lord.

I speak peace. I thank the Just Judge. I thank You, Jesus, the author and the finisher of our faith, for the Crowns of Righteousness and the Crown of Love that trump this inferior crown.

As a governing son, I pick up these Superior Crowns, place them upon our heads, and ask you to help us rule. I commission the angels to render these righteous verdicts in the spirit and the natural. I commission the angels to put this on record.

Thank you, Just Judge, for honoring us and trusting us with the responsibility of wearing this Crown of Love and Crown of Righteousness. Thank you for helping us occupy the territory you assigned us. I don't take this lightly; I ask for supernatural assistance and help daily to govern well as Your sons in the name of Jesus.

As a son, I call in the treasure lost from the north, the south, the east, and the west in every age, realm, dimension, and time to fill the capacity of this section.

I ask that all of this be done in time and out of time, and in every age, realm, and dimension, and timeline, and that all of the spiritual debris, residue, and essences that were left behind by this inferior crown and the spirits that came with it be destroyed utterly. I thank You, Father, for what you did, Jesus, for giving us authority and dominion here.

Court Case for the Removal of the Crown of Fear Off of Someone

Father, I ask to step into Your Court of Mercy to receive mercy in our time of need on behalf of _____. I ask that their generations be brought into this Court and those related to them by blood, marriage, adoption, civil or religious covenant, from Your hand in the garden and as far forward as far as it needs to go, as well as their cloud of witnesses.

Father, I present to you, _____ and their generations, and every one of them who ever wore this inferior crown, who willingly took this Crown of Fear, who even distributed it to other people in their family and their generations, and even those outside of their generations where I they instilled fear, presented fear, where they were a part of fear, where they perpetuated fear throughout the generational line, or accepted it, bent their knee to it, or even relished in, or relished it in others. Forgive them, Lord; I repent on their behalf. I ask for the blood of Jesus to be applied to this.

I am requesting that this inferior crown be removed from them and their generational line, as it pierced their heads. I ask that the angels remove this crown (even though it is not easily taken off), along with every binding and every structure that would keep it upon their heads. I request that the Crown of Fear be removed and destroyed.

I ask that the Superior Crown of Love be placed upon their heads to heal any woundedness and begin to mend their minds and the places of woundedness.

I ask that the technology of the Crowns of Sonship that they wear and the new day would infiltrate and destroy the technology of the Crown of Fear and that the nanotechnology of Jesus—of His love (for He has not given them the spirit of fear, but of power) and that the power and the dominion of the Superior Crown crush and destroy the inferior Crown of Fear.

Father has not given us the spirit of fear but of love. That love is the Supreme Crown over this inferior crown, and as the Crown of a Sound Mind is placed upon their heads, that it heals every wound of the mind and that the poison that came with that inferior Crown of Fear be drawn up out of them as they are made new.

I commission the angels to clean up the spiritual debris, residue, and essences that the spirit of fear has left behind, so they receive the Superior Crown from Jesus—

the Crown of Love, and the Crown of Power—the dominion over this, and the Crown of a Sound Mind. Thank you, Lord.

I come out of agreement with every form of superiority of the inferior Crown of Fear. They do not agree with it, and I do not either. Where they and their generations agreed and where they were lied to, and they believed that there was nothing they could do because they were so gripped by fear; that is a lie. I come out of agreement with the lie of this inferior Crown of Fear. I ask for the cancellation and annulment of these lies.

I commission the angels to capture every demonic spirit that came with the spirit of fear that came through the back door of this as it opened up the door to other spirits.

I commission the angels to gather up these spirits and take them to be judged—those that infiltrated the mind and the heart, those that brought the lies and instilled the fear.

Father, I ask in the Courts of Heaven that these inferior spirits be judged on behalf of the sons. I receive Your righteous verdicts on behalf of them and their generations. I ask that these inferior crowns be destroyed.

Thank you for the Crown of a New Day—your new for us. Thank you for the Superior Crown of the mind of Christ and the Crown of Love. Thank You, Jesus.

I ask Father for the healing balm for the wounds, for when this inferior Crown of Fear is placed on people's heads, it creates ugly wounds.

Further, I request that the name and blood of Jesus destroy this throne, mantle, and crown.

I come out of agreement with the master of this crown. Forgive us where they traded and agreed with it.

I ask that you please destroy and burn this inferior crown set on the seven-headed dragon, the dragon, its seven heads, its inferior crowns, thrones, mantles, scepters, altars, spiritual residue, essences, and debris, in Jesus' name.

I ask that the Superior Crowns of the Kingdom of Heaven be placed upon our heads, overturning the enormity of our sins.

I ask for renewed authorization for every crown restored to us and those to be restored today in Your court, as well as the release of every mantle, throne, scepter, altar, anointing, and Glory.

Your Honor, I respectfully request Your righteous verdict or further guidance.

> [If further counsel is advised, follow these instructions. Once you have received a righteous verdict, begin the following segment:]

I speak to the earth that every one of their generations who stepped upon you, even those related to them by blood, marriage, adoption, civil or religious covenant.

Earth, I have received a righteous verdict from the Courts of Heaven this day. I bless you to hear the word of the Lord. I bless you to swallow up the iniquity and the egregious sins of self-deception and wearing these inferior crowns. Swallow up every word and deed that was done upon you. Swallow the innocent bloodshed, sexual sins, moving of the boundary stones, worship of themselves, idol worship, occultic worship, theft...every sin under the sun that Jesus died for. I charge you to swallow it up and bless you to your original design. I bless you to see the governing sons and to begin blessing them. Begin pouring out your riches of abundance of truth and life.

I request the blood of Jesus to cover every place this was done upon you or in you. I speak to the frequencies of the wind to blow away the evil, to the water to drown it, and to the fire to burn it. I speak to you to return to your original design as the Lord had created you. The Earth is the Lord's, and its fullness belongs to the Lord.

I speak peace. I thank the Just Judge. I thank You, Jesus, the author and the finisher of our faith, for the Crowns of Righteousness and the Crown of Love that trump this inferior crown.

As a governing son, I pick up these Superior Crowns, place them upon our heads, and ask you to help them rule. I commission the angels to render these righteous verdicts in the spirit and the natural. I commission the angels to put this on record.

Thank you, Just Judge, for honoring me and trusting me and them with the responsibility of wearing these Crowns of Love and Crowns of Righteousness. Thank you for helping them occupy the territory you assigned them. I don't take this lightly; ask for supernatural assistance and help daily to govern well as Your sons in the name of Jesus.

As a son, I call in the treasure lost from the north, the south, the east, and the west in every age, realm, dimension, and time to fill the capacity of this section.

I ask that all of this be done in time and out of time, and in every age, realm, and dimension, and that all of the spiritual debris, residue, and essences that were left behind by this inferior crown and the spirits that came with it be destroyed utterly. I thank You, Father, for what you did, Jesus, for giving us authority and dominion here.

———— ∞ ————

Chapter 9
The False Crown of Magic

This crown is unusually beautiful and alluring. It appeared as a crown with purple stones mounted on it. The stones were a most beautiful color, purple. The crown the stones were mounted on was also beautiful, dark, and larger than the other crowns. This was important because from the back of the crown to the front, the stones were all the same size except for the one in the very front. The others were all mounted on different points, except the center stone. The middle point at the front of the crown was higher and had a beautiful, long, elongated purple stone, whereas all other stones were shorter.

The enemy doesn't trust anyone, so the larger stone embedded in this crown was the eye for him to see what they did for him. It's like back-and-forth messaging. Because he doesn't trust anyone, he sets up a monitoring system in each crown. It is wicked technology.

Although its beauty is enchanting, it is not a suitable crown. It seems to have good, but the good is contaminated by darkness and falsehood. This is the *Crown of Magic*. It is the crown on the fifth head of the dragon.

It is tantalizing, which makes this crown unique. It is a deception that comes with witchcraft. This crown is unique unto itself.

The deception here is that many believe some forms of witchcraft are good.

We saw this culturally a few years ago with the popularity of the Harry Potter series. Years before, we were socially inoculated by the television show *Bewitched*. Growing up, we were taught the false narrative of a good witch versus an evil witch in the movie *The Wizard of Oz*. We have been pre-conditioned to the lie that there is good witchcraft and evil witchcraft. NO! It is all bad!

The brides of Satan wear this crown. It has an allure, and it lures people in. It is full of lust for power. Many online games play on this theme. It has an elevation. This crown suspends those who wear it. They are in a realm of darkness that looks like light to them. It feels like power. It entices their senses, and it is full of greed.

It is the most dishonoring of crowns as dishonor alights upon the heads of those that wear it, for they have indeed dishonored the Lord. Wearers of it won't mind dishonoring those around them, especially those in authority over them. They feel justified in doing so because of their pride.

This crown has elements of truth that pull people in.

When a lie is embedded in the truth, it makes it all a lie.

The Spirit of Whoring

The spirit of whoring is with this crown. It has an insatiable appetite and is handcrafted in the depths of hell. I did a quick check with ChatGPT, and it had a surprisingly good description.

The "spirit of whoring" is a biblical and spiritual term that comes up primarily in the Old Testament, often used by the prophets when addressing Israel's unfaithfulness to God. It's not just about physical immorality—it carries a much broader and weightier meaning.

The "spirit of whoring" (sometimes translated as a "spirit of harlotry" or "spiritual adultery") refers to **a heart posture that turns away from intimacy and covenant with God to chase after other lovers—** whether those be idols, false gods, material things, ungodly alliances, or even our own desires and ambitions that pull us out of alignment with Him.

Hosea 4:12: (ESV) says:

For a spirit of whoredom has led them astray, and they have left their God to play the whore. (ESV)

- It's a metaphor, yes, but one that highlights **relational betrayal**. God isn't distant or indifferent; He's a covenantal God. So, when His people pursue other sources of provision, protection, or pleasure instead of Him, it's seen as a deep relational wound.

Characteristics of a "spirit of whoring":

- **Chronic unfaithfulness** – a pattern of turning to anything but God for identity, comfort, or security.
- **Restlessness or spiritual wandering** – never quite satisfied, always looking for something else to fulfill.
- **Transactional mindset** – treating God like a vending machine rather than a covenant partner.
- **Idolatry** – not always statues or temples, but things like fame, money, relationships, or self-will that take center stage in the heart.

- **Emotional detachment from God** – going through the motions without true affection or reverence.

Why it matters:

This spirit is so serious because it directly undermines the **intimacy and loyalty** that God desires with His people. It fractures trust, distorts identity, and opens doors to deception and spiritual compromise.

But here's the beautiful, redemptive thread: God's response is never just wrath—it's a passionate plea for return. Hosea, for example, isn't just a rebuke; it's a love story of a faithful God calling His unfaithful people back to Himself with compassion and grace. When a "spirit of whoring" creeps into the marketplace, it can undermine God-given assignments and create subtle but powerful misalignments.

How the Spirit of Whoring Affects Kingdom Businesses

A business, when stewarded by a believer, becomes an extension of covenant—a vessel through which the values, strategies, and presence of Heaven can manifest. But when the spirit of whoring infiltrates a business, that enterprise begins to drift from purpose to performance, from stewardship to striving, and from divine strategy to worldly compromise.

Here's how this shows up in practical, yet deeply spiritual ways:

1. Compromised Core Values

The business may start with a pure mandate—serving people, glorifying God, solving real problems—but along the way, decisions begin to favor profit over integrity, or visibility over obedience.

You'll hear things like:

- *"We need to be more like the world to reach the world."*
- *"Let's soften the message—it's too confrontational."*
- *"I know it's not ideal, but we have to do this to stay afloat."*

These are subtle compromises that, over time, can lead to spiritual decay.

---

2. Idolatry of Success

When accolades, revenue, followers, or recognition become the primary goal, business owners can find themselves unintentionally serving Mammon instead of the Master. It becomes less about hosting God's presence and more about "building a brand."

---

3. Misplaced Trust

Instead of consulting Heaven, decisions are made based on trends, gurus, and what the culture demands. Partnerships are formed without prayer. Systems are implemented for efficiency that don't carry God's presence. It's like digging broken cisterns that can hold no water.

4. Manipulative Marketing

The spirit of whoring can manifest in how a business attracts customers—using fear, guilt, or exaggeration to get a sale rather than walking in truth and trust. There's no rest, just endless hustle.

5. Loss of Covenant Flow

Because a covenant with God releases divine provision, guidance, and favor, stepping outside of it often results in striving, scarcity, burnout, or confusion. The business may "work" on paper, but spiritually it's dry—and owners often feel it deeply.

Repentance for Where the Spirit of Whoredoms has Crept in

I request access to the Court of Cancellations.

Father, I repent for every way I have let my business be led by fear, performance, or worldly systems. I repent for aligning with the spirit of whoring—where I have run to other sources instead of You.

I request from the Court of Cancellations the destruction of every false covenant, every allegiance with Mammon, compromise, control, or deception. I come out of agreement with the lie that success requires me to sacrifice my obedience.

I choose covenant over compromise. I choose You.

Father, I re-dedicate this business to You. It is not mine—it is Yours. I place the ownership, the decisions, the finances, and the future back in Your hands.

Give me Heaven's strategies. Let this business flow from intimacy, not ambition. Let every client, product, service, and decision honor You.

I receive Your favor, Your blueprint, and Your presence. Let my business be a dwelling place for You.

I declare:

My business is in covenant with the Living God. I will not serve two masters. I will not partner with fear.

I walk in rest, clarity, integrity, and supernatural provision. Heaven is my supply. Wisdom is my strategy. Favor is my portion.

I am aligned. I am whole. I am faithful. And my business will bear fruit that remains.

The Generational Impact of Crowns

Many of these crowns come through the assignments on the generational line, where there has been a lot of witchcraft.

We must remove these crowns from their generational line that came through bloodline iniquity and sin. Then, commission the angels to go and *blight* these crowns from the generational line. It is a blight in the bloodline where these crowns come from. To blight something is essentially to smite it from the generational lines. Many lingering human spirits are attached to the generational line because of this crown.

When you remove the crowns through repentance, you remove the lingering human spirits who wear them. There's going to be a fight about it. They're not going to want to relinquish them. They have been empowered by these crowns operating on and through the generational line. However, they will be removed.

Know that blight is something that destroys or impairs. When that crown is on the bloodline, it seeks to destroy. Remember, light dispels the darkness.

> *This crown also has a throne*
> *that needs to be dismantled.*
> *It is very much like an altar.*

Identifying the False Crown of Magic

- Have they embraced Harry Potter and other forms of witchcraft that they have no problem with?
- Is greed a problem with them?
- Do they have sexual issues?
- Do they have problems with lingering human spirits?
- Are they distrustful?
- Do they have an insatiable appetite for things?

How Do These Characteristics Affect Businesses

These characteristics speak to **open doors** that can affect the spiritual, ethical, and even financial health of a business. When these traits or issues are present in leaders or cultures, they don't just create dysfunction, they invite **spiritual contamination** that can subtly or overtly derail a Kingdom assignment.

Let's unpack each one and explore the potential **negative impact on a business**:

---

1. Have they embraced Harry Potter and other forms of witchcraft that they have no problem with?

Impact: This may seem harmless on the surface to some, but when someone embraces media or practices rooted in **occult themes**, it can desensitize the spirit to what is holy. In a Kingdom business, this opens doors to **confusion, spiritual dullness, and counterfeit revelation**. It compromises discernment and invites the influence of deception and divination. Over time, this can lead to spiritual mixture and loss of authority in prayer or decision-making.

---

2. Is greed a problem with them?

Impact: Greed replaces stewardship with **exploitation**. It drives decisions that prioritize profit over people and personal gain over Kingdom impact. Greed-driven leadership fosters environments of competition rather than collaboration, hoarding rather than generosity, and manipulation rather than ministry. It also invites Mammon into the business, which competes with God for lordship.

---

3. Do they have sexual issues?

Impact: Sexual compromise—whether hidden or public—introduces **defilement and instability** into the business. It distorts relationships, opens demonic access points, and grieves the Spirit. Leaders operating under sexual sin often also walk in shame, secrecy, or manipulation, creating unsafe emotional or spiritual environments. Trust erodes. The business may grow externally but **rot internally.**

---

4. Do they have problems with lingering human spirits?

Impact: Lingering human spirits (unclean spirits tied to the deceased or trauma) create **spiritual interference**. They can cloud discernment, introduce oppression, or even empower false prophetic experiences. If these spirits are present and not dealt with, they anchor the business in unresolved grief, trauma, or deception—the result: Strange confusion, irrational fear, or unexplained cycles of loss and instability.

---

5. Are they distrustful?

Impact: Distrust is often rooted in **past wounds, betrayal, or experiences of control.** A distrustful leader micromanages, isolates, and withholds. This stifles team synergy and damages relational trust. Employees don't feel safe or seen. Distrust limits delegation and breeds suspicion—blocking the flow of honor and collaboration that's vital for healthy, Kingdom-minded leadership.

6. Do they have an insatiable appetite for things?

Impact: This is a spirit of **lust**—not always sexual, but insatiable hunger for more. It shows up as materialism, gluttony, or status obsession. It leads to overspending, overextending, over-promising, and under-delivering. This "more-more-more" mindset pushes the business off God's timetable and into cycles of burnout, overproduction, and emptiness. It can also expose the business to **manipulative marketing or overpricing**, violating ethical principles.

Final Thoughts:

Each of these traits represents a **spiritual fracture or open gate**. Left unchecked, they allow unclean influences to distort what should be holy, causing:

- Disrupted discernment
- Strained team dynamics
- Unfruitful financial decisions
- Oppression in the atmosphere
- Weak spiritual authority
- Loss of divine favor and flow

These aren't just behavior issues; they're spiritual realities that affect **the whole business ecosystem.**

Personal Court Case
for Removal of the Crown of Magic

Father, I ask to step into Your Court of Mercy, through Jesus, on behalf of me and my generations. I ask that the accuser of the brethren be brought in as well as our generational line, from both sides of the family, and those who are with us by blood, marriage, adoption, civil or religious covenant, from Your hand in the garden and all the way forward as far as it needs to go, as well as my cloud of witnesses.

Your Honor, I agree with the adversary that we were deceived by magic and everything it encompasses.

I repent for magic, for the use of it, for the places in the generations that yielded to it, utilized it, for those who took it up, who felt empowered by it, who were deceived because of it, and for those who elevated themselves in believing the lie.

I repent for those in the generations who practiced magic but also deceived others with bits of truth to pull them into the lie. I repent on their behalf.

I repent on behalf of everyone who believed the lie, succumbed to it, and then projected it, and perpetuated it through the generational line.

I repent for agreeing with the spirit of whoring, for trading with it, for seducing because of it, and for allowing it.

I repent for the garments they wore. I ask that they be removed and destroyed now.

I repent, sir, all the way back to Your hand in the garden and all the way forward as far as it needs to go. Father, I repent for taking this inferior crown and for the use of this crown. Where they saw it as useful, yet it was a lie.

I repent of where I have placed this inferior crown on other people's heads and our own.

On behalf of the lingering human spirits who are or who are not a part of our bloodline, as well as our generations who are now assigned to the bloodline because of taking up these inferior crowns. I repent on their behalf for every sin under the sun, which is egregious, which dishonored and brought dishonor to the Lord because of taking up and wearing these inferior crowns.

I ask the angels to open up the silver channel, take the demonic guard and the bosses who were assigned to these LHSs, to Jesus' feet for judgment. To every lingering human spirit in the generational line, you will go and see Jesus today. You are not staying.

I forgive you, bless you, and release you for what you were doing in and through the bloodline. You are removed this day by the hand of God because of repentance, which we are allowed to do. He forgave us, and I forgive you.

When you see Jesus, I suggest you ask Him for mercy. Angels, I commission you to destroy every inferior crown of witchcraft in the name of Jesus.

I ask for a Crown of Truth to be given to our generational line—the utter and distinct truth, the Superior Crown that causes all other inferior crowns to be dismantled and destroyed, as their knee must bow, in the name of Jesus.

I ask that the thrones and mantles be found, dismantled, and destroyed in every place throughout the generational line.

Where our generations set this up as a type of altar, I ask that it be destroyed, and that every attendant of every altar be captured and dealt with according to the will of the Father, and that the idol of witchcraft, as well as this Crown of Magic, be judged in the courts today.

I commission the angels to take every spirit or entity who has been assigned or associated with this throne, inferior crown, mantle, and scepter to be taken to court for judgment. I commission the angels to destroy the thrones forever, and that the altar of the Lord be established in their place, in and through the bloodline. I request that angels be assigned there to worship and that the Crown of Truth be established as it sits upon the altar of the Lord.

I request that every false scepter that came with this inferior crown and this throne, which was considered to be a wand, also be taken from the generational bloodline and be utterly destroyed, annulled, and removed. I ask that its frequency be dismantled and destroyed in the name of Jesus.

I request the realm of the inferior hovering crown, the realm from which it came, be closed, and that there be a closed, sealed door in and upon the line of the generations forevermore with no ability to reopen.

I request that the center stone of this inferior crown, which is the eye, be utterly crushed, annulled, canceled, destroyed, and blinded forever in, through, and upon the generational line.

I ask for the amendment of 'As if it Never Were.'

I ask that you please destroy and burn this inferior crown which is set on the seven-headed dragon, the dragon, its seven heads, its inferior crowns, thrones, mantles, scepters, altars, spiritual residue, essences, and debris, in Jesus' name.

I ask for the Superior Crowns of the Kingdom of Heaven to be placed on our heads, overturning the egregiousness of our sins.

I ask for renewed authorization for every crown restored to us, and those to be restored today in Your court and *the release of every mantle, throne, scepter, altar, anointing, and Glory.*

I ask for our righteous verdicts or further counsel.

> [If further counsel is advised, follow these instructions. Once you have received a righteous verdict, begin the following segment:]

I speak to the earth, water, air, and fire. I have received a righteous verdict, and since the world and the fullness of it belong to the Lord, I charge you to swallow up, drown, blow away and burn all evil words, deeds, lies, witchcraft, innocent bloodshed, sexual sins, occultic cauldrons, evil rooms, evil technologies, spells, hex's, vexes, incantations, voodoo, dark art, manipulation, monitoring, astral projections, evil projections, counterfeit intelligence, and any and all other darkness or evil done upon the earth, through the air, to the water and using fire.

I bless you to the fullness of your original design and charge you to bless us as the Lord walks through time, restoring it and you to their fullness. I do this in the name and blood of Jesus and as a governing son.

As a son, I call in the treasure that has been lost from the north, the south, the east, and the west in every age, realm, dimension, and time to fill the capacity of this section.

I ask that all of this be done in time and out of time, and in every age, realm, and dimension, and that all of the spiritual debris, residue, and essences left behind by this inferior crown and the spirits that came with it be destroyed utterly. I thank You, Father, for what you did, Jesus, for giving us authority and dominion here.

Court Case for Removal of the Crown of Magic Off of Someone

Father, I ask to step into Your Court of Mercy, through Jesus, on behalf of _____ and their generations. I ask that the accuser of the brethren be brought in as well as their generational line, from both sides of the family, and those who are with them by blood, marriage, adoption, civil or religious covenant, from Your hand in the garden and as far forward as it needs to go, as well as their cloud of witnesses.

Your Honor, I agree with the adversary that they were deceived by magic and everything it encompasses.

I repent for magic, for the use of it, for the places in their generations that yielded to it, utilized it, for those who took it up, who felt empowered by it, who were deceived because of it, and for those who elevated themselves in believing the lie.

I repent for those in their generations who practiced magic but also deceived others with bits of truth to pull them into the lie. I repent on their behalf.

I repent on behalf of everyone in their generations who believed the lie, succumbed to it, and then projected it, and perpetuated it through the generational line.

I repent for agreeing with the spirit of whoring, for trading with it, for seducing because of it, and for allowing it.

I repent for the garments they wore. I ask that they be removed and destroyed now.

I repent, sir, all the way back to Your hand in the garden and all the way forward as far as it needs to go. Father, I repent for taking this inferior crown and for the use of this crown. Where they saw it as useful, yet it was a lie.

I repent where they put this inferior crown on other people's heads and their own.

On behalf of the lingering human spirits who are or who are not a part of our bloodline, as well as their generations who are now assigned to the bloodline because of taking up these inferior crowns. I repent on their behalf for every sin under the sun, which is egregious, which dishonored and brought dishonor to the Lord because of taking up and wearing these inferior crowns.

I commission the angels to go through the timelines, ages, and dimensions for every person who wore this inferior crown, and I commission you to take it off their heads as we stand before the Lord in repentance for them. I forgive, bless, and release them.

I ask the angels to open up the silver channel, take the demonic guard and the bosses who were assigned to these LHSs, to Jesus' feet for judgment. To every lingering human spirit in the generational line, you will go and see Jesus today. You are not staying.

I forgive you, bless you, and release you for what you were doing in and through the bloodline. You are removed this day by the hand of God because of repentance, which we are allowed to do. He forgave us, and I forgive you.

When you see Jesus, I suggest you ask Him for mercy. Angels, I commission you to destroy every inferior crown of witchcraft in the name of Jesus.

I ask for a Crown of Truth to be given to our generational line—the utter and distinct truth, the Superior Crown that causes all other inferior crowns to be dismantled and destroyed, as their knee must bow, in the name of Jesus.

I ask that the thrones and mantles be found, dismantled, and destroyed in every place throughout the generational line.

Where their generations set this up as a type of altar, I ask that it be destroyed, and that every attendant of every altar be captured and dealt with according to the will of the Father, and that the idol of witchcraft, as well as this Crown of Magic, be judged in the courts today.

I commission the angels to take every spirit or entity who has been assigned or associated with this throne, inferior crown, mantle, and scepter to be taken to court for judgment. I commission the angels to destroy the thrones forever, and that the altar of the Lord be established in their place, in and through the bloodline. I request that angels be assigned there to worship and that the Crown of Truth be established as it sits upon the altar of the Lord.

I request that every false scepter that came with this inferior crown and this throne, which was considered to be a wand, also be taken from the generational bloodline and be utterly destroyed, annulled, and removed. I ask that its frequency be dismantled and destroyed in the name of Jesus.

I request the realm of the inferior hovering crown, the realm from which it came, be closed, and that there be a closed, sealed door in and upon the line of the generations forevermore with no ability to reopen.

I request that the center stone of this inferior crown, which is the eye, be utterly crushed, annulled, canceled, destroyed, and blinded forever in, though, and upon the generational line.

I ask for the amendment of 'As if it Never Were.'

I ask that you please destroy and burn this inferior crown which is set on the seven-headed dragon, the dragon, its seven heads, its inferior crowns, thrones, mantles, scepters, altars, spiritual residue, essences, and debris, in Jesus' name.

I ask that the Superior Crowns of the Kingdom of Heaven be placed upon our heads, overturning the enormity of our sins.

I ask for renewed authorization for every crown restored to us, and those to be restored today in Your court, and the release of every mantle, throne, scepter, altar, anointing, and Glory.

I ask for our righteous verdicts or further counsel.

> [If further counsel is advised, follow these instructions. Once you have received a righteous verdict, begin the following segment:]

I speak to the earth, water, air, and fire. I have received a righteous verdict, and since the world and the fullness of it belong to the Lord, I charge you to swallow up, drown, blow away and burn all evil words, deeds, lies, witchcraft, innocent bloodshed, sexual sins, occultic cauldrons, evil rooms, evil technologies, spells, hex's, vexes, incantations, voodoo, dark art, manipulation, monitoring, astral projections, evil projections, counterfeit intelligence, and any and all other darkness or evil done upon the earth, through the air, to the water and using fire.

I bless you to the fullness of your original design and charge you to bless us as the Lord walks through time, restoring it and you to their fullness. I do this in the name and blood of Jesus and as a governing son.

As a son, I call in the treasure that has been lost from the north, the south, the east, and the west in every age, realm, dimension, and time to fill the capacity of this section.

I ask that all of this be done in time and out of time, and in every age, realm, and dimension, and that all of the spiritual debris, residue, and essences left behind by this inferior crown and the spirits that came with it be destroyed utterly. I thank You, Father, for what you did, Jesus, for giving us authority and dominion here.

───── ∞ ─────

Chapter 10
The False Crown of Secrets

This inferior crown is unlike any other. It is quiet and stealthy. It silences the sons. It is bloodthirsty, and it screams of desire to pierce frequencies, and it walks with the spirit of death. Its inner workings are harlotry, divination, and mockery.

The sounds of intercession rub and excoriate the head of this dragon, which is why it seeks to silence the sons. The Pharisees wore this crown with their lofty robes. Violence comes from the mouth of this dragon who wears this crown.

This Crown of Secrets works in tandem with the Crown of Antichrist. A cloak hides this dragon's head.

---

*This crown is the seat
of Freemasonry,
so it has a throne
and it is shrouded in secrecy.*

Degree levels of Freemasonry also have crowns. It revels in its deception. In this crown is fantasy that cooperates with harlotry. Simply look at the titles of the various degrees of Freemasonry. It's almost as if they created a weird world with fantastical titles. This is the defilement of the imagination.

This crown not only seeks silence but also mocks the sons. Its mouth is full of corruption, indignity, and falsehood. It's stealthy in nature.

Every secret will be revealed. Secrets shroud, but the uncovering is unbearable. It is the Lord who uncovers that many times.

It is this head of the dragon that seeks to shame and silence the sons. Have no secrets within you.

Recently, the pastor of a large church in the Dallas/Fort Worth area was forced to resign due to something that happened with an underage woman many years ago. His secret came out, silencing and shaming him.

Remember the old saying, "Be sure your sin will find you out, has much truth in it."

Remove and utterly destroy this crown from your heads. It is unbecoming of a son.

James 5:16:

> **_Confess your trespasses to one another_**, _and pray for one another, that you may be healed. The effective, fervent prayer of a righteous man avails much. (Emphasis mine)_

Regret is in this crown. You must crush this serpent under your feet.

Don't fall into its trap. _Govern_ this crown, _remove it_, and _destroy it_. The sons bear the responsibility of secrets.

Deuteronomy 29:29:

> _The **secret things belong to the LORD** our God, but those things which are revealed belong to us and to our children forever, that we may do all the words of this law. (Emphasis mine)_

Psalms 25:14:

> _The **secret of the LORD** is with those who fear Him, and He will show them His covenant. (Emphasis mine)_

Mark 4:22:

> _For there **is nothing that is hidden that won't be disclosed**, and **there is no secret that won't be brought out into the light!** (Emphasis mine)_

Identifying the False Crown of Secrets

- Do they appear religious on the surface?
- Do they mock believers?
- Do they seek to silence believers?
- Do they shame people?
- Do they "kick back" at the thought of intercession?
- Are they violent when challenged?
- Are they involved in Freemasonry or other secret organizations?
- Will they disparage someone of a different mindset?
- Do they appear religious on the surface?

How Do These Characteristics Affect Businesses

When these traits emerge—especially within a business intended to operate under Kingdom principles—they can create significant spiritual and cultural toxicity. Let's walk through each one, unpacking how it can **negatively impact a business**, especially one that is supposed to carry the fragrance of Christ.

---

1. Do they appear religious on the surface?

Impact: This signals *form without power* (2 Timothy 3:5). When leadership or branding has a "Christian coating" but lacks authentic spiritual depth, it creates disillusionment among employees and clients alike. It fosters performance-based environments where appearances matter more than substance. This can breed hypocrisy, hinder genuine transformation, and repel those seeking authenticity.

2. Do they mock believers?

Impact: This reveals a spirit of **contempt** for true faith. Mocking believers, especially those walking in deeper levels of intimacy or obedience, creates a culture of dishonor. It silences the voice of the Spirit and breeds fear or division among staff. It also opens the door for gossip, cynicism, and spiritual compromise in the workplace.

3. Do they seek to silence believers?

Impact: When faith expressions (like prayer, intercession, or spiritual insight) are suppressed, the business effectively cuts off Heaven's counsel. God's strategies often flow through vessels that are yielded. If believers are silenced, so too are divine wisdom, warning, and creativity. This quenching of the Spirit can cause a business to drift into confusion, make poor decisions, or even lead to disaster.

4. Do they shame people?

Impact: Shame is the currency of control, not covenant. Businesses that operate through shame (subtle or overt) create unsafe environments, where innovation dies, fear thrives, and people shrink rather than grow. It damages morale, invites turnover, and undermines Kingdom culture at its core.

5. Do they "kick back" at the thought of intercession?

Impact: Resistance to intercession often signals pride or spiritual dullness. Intercession is a lifeline of revelation and protection. The business forfeits divine insight, angelic intervention, and prophetic warning when rejected. It opens the door to demonic infiltration and blinds the leadership to spiritual realities influencing their outcomes.

6. Are they violent when challenged?

Impact: This doesn't always mean physical violence—it could be verbal abuse, intimidation, or passive-aggressive retaliation. Such responses are symptoms of a **Jezebelic or orphan spirit**—where control matters more than truth. This creates a toxic power dynamic that repels the Holy Spirit and instills fear in the team. Creativity, loyalty, and trust wither under this.

7. Are they involved in Freemasonry or other secret organizations?

Impact: These are spiritual covenants that stand in **direct opposition** to the Kingdom of God. Involvement in Freemasonry introduces oaths, bloodlines, and altars that bring **spiritual contamination.** Even unknowingly, businesses tied to these systems often experience cycles of lack, betrayal, confusion, or premature death of vision. The foundation must be broken and rebuilt in truth.

8. Will they disparage someone from a different mindset?

Impact: This reveals pride and tribalism. It creates an atmosphere where only certain voices are validated, and diversity of thought is punished. In a Kingdom business, **honor must be a core currency.** Without it, innovation stalls and relationships fracture. Disparaging others—especially those who carry different but God-ordained callings—blocks the flow of Heaven's collaborative genius.

9. (Repeat) Do they appear religious on the surface?

Impact (re-emphasized): This repetition drives home the danger of outward religiosity without inner transformation. It invites **a Pharisaical spirit**—where image is more important than truth. This alienates the broken, fosters self-righteousness, and ultimately makes the business spiritually brittle and resistant to real revival.

Final Thoughts:

When these traits are present, it's a sign that **the spirit of whoring may have gained ground**, pulling the business out of covenant and into idolatry, control, and deception. A Kingdom business must walk in **truth, honor, humility, and Spirit-led courage.** Without these, it becomes a vessel of mixture—spiritually compromised and strategically hindered.

Personal Court Case for
the Removal of the Crown of Secrets

Father, I ask to step into Your Court of Mercy, through Jesus, on behalf of me and my generations. I ask that the accuser of the brethren be brought in as well as our generational line, from both sides of the family, and those who are with us by blood, marriage, adoption, civil or religious covenant, from Your hand in the garden and all the way forward as far as it needs to go, as well as my cloud of witnesses.

I want to repent on behalf of myself and my generation, who kept secrets and took this crown willingly. I reveled in harlotry, took on shame, co-labored with deception, allowed it to mock, and caused our own silencing of Your voice. As a governing son, forgive us and our generations for the secrets and for even having secrets about other people and using those secrets against them.

I repent for not taking this crown off our own heads, not confessing our sins one to another so that we could be healed, not confessing these things to you. We harbored them in our hearts and acted like you didn't know. I repent where we acted like you couldn't see and where we kept a secret. And we even smiled about it and reveled in it.

Forgive us and our generations, and forgive us where we took the throne and the seat of Freemasonry within our generations and did not present the throne and the crown to you.

I take it, and I crush it—this inferior crown under our feet—the head of the snake, the head of this dragon, I crush it and present to you the throne and request that the angels utterly destroy it, and the altar, and the idols of secrecy be judged in Your court this day as I repent on behalf of the generations for they did not know what they were doing. I ask that a complete capture of every demonic spirit that was used be made. Forgive us where your voice through us was silenced.

Because of this, I ask that angels crush shame and regret, and I ask for the amendment of 'As if it Never Were' as your blood pours through our generations, that the angels would go and remove every single Crown of Secrets in the bloodline and destroy it.

Forgive us when we uncovered other people and brought them shame because of the secret we knew about. I accept Father the scripture that everything that is done in secret is brought to light—your light. I ask this in the name of Jesus.

I thank You, Father, I thank You, Jesus, and I thank you, John, for your transparency as we are learning that transparency is Godly—no secrets.

I repent for any and all cooperation with Baal in any form at any time. I turn our back to the altar of Baal and ask angels to destroy every altar of Baal. I ask for a divorce from Baal, Lucifer, the red dragon, the Book of Magic, and any ungodly attraction. I ask that all debris associated with this cooperation with Baal be removed and destroyed on our behalf. I remove the regalia associated with this ungodly marriage covenant and request to be clothed in robes of righteousness.

I request that the head of this snake be cut off from the other heads and from this dragon.

I ask that you please destroy and burn this inferior crown which is set on the seven-headed dragon, the dragon, its seven heads, its inferior crowns, thrones, mantles, scepters, altars, spiritual residue, essences, and debris, in Jesus' name.

I ask for the Superior Crowns of the Kingdom of Heaven to be placed on our heads, overturning the egregiousness of our sins.

I ask for renewed authorization for every crown restored to us, and those to be restored today in Your court, and the release of every mantle, throne, scepter, altar, anointing, and Glory.

I ask for Your righteous verdict or further counsel.

> [If further counsel is advised, follow these instructions. Once you have received a righteous verdict, begin the following segment:]

I speak to the earth that every one of our generations who stepped upon you, even those related to us by blood, marriage, adoption, civil or religious covenant.

Earth, I have received a righteous verdict from the Courts of Heaven this day. I bless you to hear the word of the Lord. I bless you to swallow up the iniquity and the egregious sins of self-deception and wearing these inferior crowns. Swallow up every word and deed that was done upon you. Swallow the innocent bloodshed, sexual sins, moving of the boundary stones, worship of ourselves, idol worship, occultic worship, theft…every sin under the sun that Jesus died for. I charge you to swallow it up and bless you to your original design. I bless you to see the governing sons and to begin blessing us. Begin pouring out your riches of abundance of truth and life.

I request the blood of Jesus to cover every place this was done upon you or in you. I speak to the frequencies of the wind to blow away the evil, to the water to drown it, and to the fire to burn it. I speak to you to return to your original design as the Lord had created you. The Earth is the Lord's, and its fullness belongs to the Lord.

I speak peace. I thank the Just Judge. I thank You, Jesus, the author and the finisher of our faith, for the Crowns of Righteousness and the Crown of Love that trump this inferior crown.

As a governing son, I pick up these Superior Crowns, place them upon our heads, and ask you to help us rule. I commission the angels to render these righteous verdicts in the spirit and the natural. I commission the angels to put this on record.

Thank you, Just Judge, for honoring us and trusting us with the responsibility of wearing these Crowns of Love and Righteousness. Thank you for helping us occupy the territory you assigned us. I don't take this lightly and ask for supernatural assistance and help daily to govern well as Your sons, in the name of Jesus.

As a son, I call in the treasure that has been lost from the north, the south, the east, and the west in every age, realm, dimension, and time to fill the capacity of this section.

I ask that all of this be done in time and out of time, and in every age, realm, and dimension, and that all of the spiritual debris, residue, and essences that were left behind by this inferior crown and the spirits that came with it be destroyed utterly. Thank You, Father, for what you did, Jesus, for giving us authority and dominion here.

Court Case for the Removal of the Crown of Secrets Off of Someone

Father, I ask to step into Your Court of Mercy, on behalf of _____ through Jesus, on behalf of them and their generations.

I ask that the accuser of the brethren be brought in as well as our generational line, from both sides of the family, and those who are with us by blood, marriage, adoption, civil or religious covenant, from Your hand in the garden and all the way forward as far as it needs to go, as well as my cloud of witnesses.

I want to repent on behalf of them and their generations, who kept secrets and took this crown willingly. They reveled in harlotry, took on shame, co-labored with deception, allowed it to mock, and caused their silencing of Your voice. As a governing son, forgive them and their *generations for the secrets and for even having secrets about other people and using those secrets against them.*

I repent on their behalf for them not taking this crown off their own heads, not confessing their sins one to another so that they could be healed, not confessing these things to you. They harbored them in their hearts and acted like you didn't know. I repent where they acted like you couldn't see, and where they kept secrets. And they even smiled about it and reveled in it.

Forgive them and their generations, and forgive them where they took the throne and the seat of Freemasonry within their generations and did not present the throne and the crown to you.

As a governing son, I take it and I crush this inferior crown under their feet—I crush the head of this dragon and present to you the throne and request that the angels utterly destroy it, the altar(s), and the idols of secrecy. May they be judged in Your court this day as I repent on behalf of them and their generations, for they did not know what they were doing. I ask for a complete capture of every demonic spirit that was used. Forgive us where your voice through them was silenced.

Because of this, I ask that angels crush shame and regret, and I ask for the amendment of 'As if it Never Were' as your blood pours through their generations, that the angels would go and remove every single Crown of Secrets in the bloodline and destroy it.

Forgive them when they uncovered other people and brought them shame because of the secret they knew about them. Father, I accept the scripture that everything that is done in secret is brought to light—your light. I ask this in the name of Jesus.

I repent for all cooperation with Baal in any form at any time. I turn our back to the altar of Baal and ask angels to destroy every altar of Baal. I ask for a divorce from Baal, Lucifer (Helel),[5] the red dragon, the Book of Magic, and any ungodly attraction. I ask that all debris associated with this cooperation with Baal be removed and destroyed on their behalf. I remove the regalia associated with this ungodly marriage covenant and request to be clothed in robes of righteousness.

I request that the head of this snake be cut off from the other heads and this dragon.

I ask that you please destroy and burn this inferior crown which is set on the seven-headed dragon, the dragon, its seven heads, its inferior crowns, thrones, mantles, scepters, altars, spiritual residue, essences, and debris, in Jesus' name.

---

[5] The name "Lucifer" in Isaiah 14:12 comes from the Latin Vulgate translation, not the original Hebrew text as translated by Jerome. The Hebrew word is "helel" which means "shining one" or "morning star." It comes from the root word "halal" meaning "to shine" or "to boast."

I ask that the Superior Crowns of the Kingdom of Heaven be placed upon our heads, overturning the enormity of our sins.

I ask for renewed authorization for every crown restored to us, and those to be restored today in Your court, and the release of every mantle, throne, scepter, altar, anointing, and Glory.

I ask for Your righteous verdict or further counsel.

> [If further counsel is advised, follow these instructions. Once you have received a righteous verdict, begin the following segment:]

I speak to the earth that every one of their generations who stepped upon you, even those related to them by blood, marriage, adoption, civil or religious covenant.

Earth, I have received a righteous verdict from the Courts of Heaven this day. I bless you to hear the word of the Lord. I bless you to swallow up the iniquity and the egregious sins of self-deception and wearing these inferior crowns. Swallow up every word and deed that was done upon you. Swallow the innocent bloodshed, sexual sins, moving of the boundary stones, worship of ourselves, idol worship, occultic worship, theft...every sin under the sun that Jesus died for. I charge you to swallow it up and bless you to your original design. I bless you to see the governing sons and to begin blessing them. Begin pouring out your riches of abundance of truth and life.

I request the blood of Jesus to cover every place this was done upon you or in you. I speak to the frequencies of the wind to blow away the evil, to the water to drown it, and to the fire to burn it. I speak to you to return to your original design as the Lord had created you. The Earth is the Lord's, and its fullness belongs to the Lord.

I speak peace to you. I thank the Just Judge. I thank You, Jesus, the author and the finisher of our faith, for the Crowns of Righteousness and the Crown of Love that trump this inferior crown.

As a governing son, I pick up these Superior Crowns, place them upon their heads, and ask you to help them rule. I commission the angels to render these righteous verdicts in the spirit and the natural. I commission the angels to put this on record.

Thank you, Just Judge, for honoring us and trusting us with the responsibility of wearing these Crowns of Love and Righteousness. Thank you for helping us occupy the territory you assigned us. I don't take this lightly and ask for supernatural assistance and help daily to govern well as Your sons, in the name of Jesus.

As a son, I call in the treasure that has been lost to them and their generations from the north, the south, the east, and the west in every age, realm, dimension, and time to fill the capacity of this section.

I ask that all of this be done in time and out of time, and in every age, realm, and dimension, and that all of the spiritual debris, residue, and essences that were left behind by this inferior crown and the spirits that came with it be destroyed utterly. Thank You, Father, for what you did, Jesus, for giving us authority and dominion here.

However, Mark 4:22 says:

*For there **is nothing that is hidden that won't be disclosed,** and **there is no secret that won't be brought out into the light!** (Emphasis mine)*

Instructions to the Sons:

- Remove and utterly destroy this crown from your heads. It is unbecoming of a son.
- Repent for any involvement with this crown at any time, in any fashion, in any place.
- You are to govern this crown, then remove it, then destroy it.
- Crush this serpent under your feet.

———— ∞ ————

Chapter 11

The False Crown of Antichrist

This crown is full of pomp and circumstance. There is an *elitism* to those who wear this crown. They have a 'Better than you' attitude." It looks down at people.

It has an air of superiority and a superiority complex, not unlike the Sadducees and teachers of the Law in the New Testament. This is the crown that the antichrist will wear.

Those who wear this crown *are indoctrinated*. It has multiple purposes. It works with the Crown of Secrets and the Crown of Deceit, and those who wear it can easily put on the Crown of Deception.

This crown clings to the cross, but in a defiled manner. It is superstitious, seeks fame, is pretentious, full of pride, lofty, arrogant, and judgmental. This crown *has infiltrated the church*. This crown calls in the Delilahs, the Jezebels, and the Ahab's. It has the deadliest bite. In its bite, there are many poisons. This crown *has led more astray* than any of the other crowns. That's what makes it noteworthy. This is the Crown of Antichrist. It embodies false religion. It has a realm.

> *It is the Crown of Antichrist,*
> *there is a Realm of Antichrist*
> *and a Spirit of Antichrist*
> *as well as an Office of Antichrist.*

Many would believe that the unsaved wear this crown, but it is upon those in the church, those with the deadly bite, and upon those who co-conspire with the *spirit*, the *office*, and the *realm* of the antichrist.

It has polluted the church—the ecclesia. Those who are bitten by those who wear this crown often leave the Body of Christ and never return. Over the last several years, you have probably heard or been aware of pastors who have suddenly announced they no longer believe in God. They have taken this crown.

> *Its main goal and focus*
> *are to bring an end*
> *to the embodiment of the church.*

It wants to stop the church dead in its tracks. It will convince people that what Jesus did on the cross and at the resurrection was insufficient. It tells you that Jesus might do it for someone else, but it won't work for you. It denies the power of the resurrection, although it pretends to believe in the power of the resurrection.

To deal with it,
remove not only its mantle,
the crown, and its seat,
which is a throne,
but also the Delilahs.

The Delilahs aim to undermine the influence of those working for the Kingdom. It wants them to become eunuchs.

Focus on repentance on behalf of those in the body of Christ who have been elevated to positions and seats of power, and those who have tolerated Jezebel.[6] *Close the portal, remove its garments (false mantles), and request that the head of this snake be cut off from the rest.* It empowers and emboldens those whose lust is power and greed, and it enslaves those under it.

---

[6] See Revelation 2:20 – toleration of Jezebel implies toleration of sexual sin in essentially any form, self-gratification, pornography, fornication, adultery, incest, homosexuality, bestiality, etc.

> *You must break off the chains of enslavement from this crown for the people.*

It may appear harmless on the surface, but its bite is deadly and poisonous. It will weave a web of lies and suggest weaknesses in those who lead the Body of Christ, implying that God has specially anointed them to fix all the problems in their church. They are cunning and beguiling.

One of the ways it operates in conjunction with the Crown of Secrets is through the infiltration of Freemasonry and the Eastern Star within the church. Many spiritual leaders, pastors, and clergy are Freemasons or are involved in the Eastern Star. This spirit will reach over and place the Crown of Deceit or Deception on people's heads.

This crown has an office, too—the Office of the Crown of Antichrist. This crown is specifically designed to work in conjunction with the Crown of Secrets and the Crown of Deceit or Deception. It will cause you to be delusional, have delusions of grandeur, and be secretive. How many pastors and how many churches have been covered in secrets?"

If you have found yourself involved in a church that is secretive, understand that a common secret that churches infiltrated by Freemasonry have is that of child abuse and pedophilia. You want to remove yourself from that environment as quickly as possible. They will attempt to keep you in the circle by offering positions of power within the church, but it is merely a means to ensnare you.

It's not just about removing this crown; you must *remove its mantle, destroy the seat,* and *close the portal,* for it opens portals of deception within the church. It self-justifies the abuse of children as some perverted duty of the adults (particularly the men). You must *break the chains from those who have been impacted or who have been in agreement with one who wears this crown,* and *those who were over you.*

This may involve ownership claims upon those who have become victims of their wicked works, which you can resolve in the Court of Titles and Deeds. Pay attention to sudden behavioral changes in your children. These often indicate some secretive behavior has affected them. Waste no time in excising yourself from a church environment such as this.

Identifying the False Crown of Antichrist

- Do I believe I'm spiritually superior to others?
- Do I carry a "better than you" attitude toward employees, clients, or other leaders?
- Do I crave recognition, titles, or position above intimacy with God?

- Do I look down on those who don't share my level of knowledge, influence, or "anointing"?
- Have I ever pretended to follow Christ externally while secretly doubting His power or sufficiency?
- Do I cling to religious symbols (like the cross) while harboring judgment, legalism, or bitterness?
- Do I preach grace while practicing control?
- Have I excused sin under the banner of spiritual "responsibility" or "maturity"?

How Do These Characteristics Affect Businesses

When these underlying attitudes show up in a business environment, particularly in a **Kingdom-based or spiritually aligned business**, they can **corrupt the atmosphere, undermine leadership integrity,** and **block the flow of revelation, trust, and favor.** Let's walk through each one and explore its negative impact on a business.

1. Do I believe I'm spiritually superior to others?

Impact: This creates a **toxic spiritual hierarchy** where humility and teachability are lost. Employees and clients will feel condescended to or judged rather than served and honored. It shuts down collaboration, breeds resentment, and creates an unsafe emotional and spiritual environment.

2. Do I carry a "better than you" attitude toward employees, clients, or other leaders?

Impact: This fosters division, discouragement, and silent rebellion. It undermines team cohesion and blocks the very culture Kingdom businesses are called to cultivate—**honor, unity, and empowerment**. People won't grow under you; they'll shrink—or leave.

3. Do I crave recognition, titles, or position above intimacy with God?

Impact: This reflects a **performance-driven culture** that prioritizes human praise over God's approval. It results in burnout, superficial success, and spiritually dry leadership. The business may grow numerically, but it will lack true Kingdom fruit.

4. Do I look down on those who don't share my level of knowledge, influence, or "anointing"?

Impact: This attitude fosters elitism, stifling servant leadership and silencing valuable voices. Clients and team members may be dismissed or devalued, causing missed opportunities for creativity, innovation, and divine collaboration.

5. Have I ever pretended to follow Christ externally while secretly doubting His power or sufficiency?

Impact: This creates a **split between form and power**—a dangerous spiritual hypocrisy. It invites mixture, undermines integrity, and opens the door to counterfeit solutions. The business loses its spiritual authority and Heaven's backing, even if its external image remains polished.

6. Do I cling to religious symbols (like the cross) while harboring judgment, legalism, or bitterness?

Impact: This fosters a **false sense of holiness** that repels the very people the business is called to serve. It produces a culture of fear instead of grace, and control instead of liberty. It can also **harden hearts** and blind leaders to their own need for repentance and growth.

7. Do I preach grace while practicing control?

Impact: This kind of duplicity confuses and wounds people. It creates cognitive dissonance in teams and clients alike, damaging trust. People may stay out of fear or obligation, but **their hearts will not be aligned**, and the atmosphere will become spiritually oppressive.

8. Have I excused sin under the banner of spiritual "responsibility" or "maturity"?

Impact: This opens a gateway to **spiritual abuse and manipulation**. When leaders cloak personal compromise in religious language, it undermines credibility and fosters a culture where deception and compromise are normalized. Long-term, it leads to scandal, mass disillusionment, and the crumbling of the business's spiritual foundation.

Final Thoughts:

These characteristics, if not confronted, create a **False Crown culture**—one marked by pride, pretense, and power rather than humility, authenticity, and servanthood. They **grieve the Holy Spirit**, invite spiritual confusion, and lead to the erosion of God-given vision.

Steps to Freedom
from the Crown of Antichrist.

In order to remove this crown, you must:

1. Remove its mantle.
2. Destroy the seat.

3. Close the portal.
4. Break the chains.

Personal Court Case for the Removal of the Crown of Antichrist

Father, I ask to step into the Mercy Court of Heaven to receive Mercy in our time of need. I request the accuser of the brethren be brought in as well as my entire generations and everyone related to me by blood, marriage, adoption, civil or religious covenant, from Your hand in the garden, and all the way forward as far as it needs to go, as well as my cloud of witnesses.

Your Honor, I agree with the adversary that my generations bowed our knees to this dragon, accepted the inferior crowns, and wore them proudly. I repent for the spirit of antichrist we bore and the inferior crown we took upon our heads. I repent for the pomp and circumstance, elitism, better than you attitude, superiority complex, indoctrination we took on, as well as the indoctrination of others; I repent for embodying a false religion and for 'biting' those we were in stewardship over, releasing the poison. I repent for working with the false Crown of Delusion as well as the false Crown of Secrets. I repent for all of the secrets this inferior crown bore that we agreed with.

I repent for conspiring with the office, realm, and spirit of antichrist, for embodying it. I repent for participating in exploiting, polluting, and poisoning the church, the body, and the ecclesia. I repent for being a part of ending the lives of bodies of ecclesias, people, and churches. I repent for allowing, tolerating, being in league with, and cooperating with the Delilah spirit, Jezebel, and Ahab. I repent for opening up an evil portal and for creating evil timelines for us, our generations, and for others. I repent for taking on this mantle, sitting in the seat of office, and ruling unjustly over your people. I repent for seeking to be elevated to positions and seats of power, or where we, who wore this inferior crown, elevated those who should never have been elevated. I repent for the pride and for lusting after power and greed.

I repent for the false clinging to the cross, the defilement and mockery of it, for seeking fame, being pretentious, full of pride, lofty, arrogant, and judging others. I repent for embodying false religion, for promoting and esteeming it. Forgive us and our generations for infiltrating the church, bringing this inferior crown and elevating others to it. Forgive us for leading others astray.

I request your blood, Jesus, the amendment of 'As If It Never Were', the destruction of the seat/office/throne, the closing of the portal, and the removal of the garments. Please remove its mantle, destroy the seat, and close the portal. I ask that you break the chains from those who have been impacted or who have agreed with those who have worn this inferior crown over the generations, and from those whom we have oppressed. Please have these destroyed.

I request that the chains attached to us and our generations be cut, severed, destroyed, dismantled, and the ashes of them be brought to Jesus. I request a complete destruction, annulment, cancellation, and overturning of the office of the Crown of Antichrist, in the name of Jesus.

I also request that the angels clean up the spiritual debris, essences, and residues in time, out of time, and in every age, realm, and dimension to infinity. Burn it and give the ashes to Jesus.

I ask that you please destroy and burn this inferior crown which is set on the seven-headed dragon, the dragon, its seven heads, its inferior crowns, thrones, mantles, scepters, altars, spiritual residue, essences, and debris, in Jesus' name.

I ask that the Superior Crowns of the Kingdom of Heaven be placed upon our heads, overturning the enormity of our sins.

I ask for renewed authorization for every crown restored to us, and those to be restored today in Your court, and the release of every mantle, throne, scepter, altar, anointing, and Glory.

I ask for Your righteous verdict or further counsel.

[If further repentance is needed, follow the instructions of the court.]

With our righteous verdict in hand, I speak to the Earth. I speak to you that every one of our generations who stepped upon you, even those related to us by blood, marriage, adoption, civil or religious covenant. Earth, I have received a righteous verdict from the Courts of Heaven this day.

I bless you to hear the word of the Lord. I bless you to swallow up the iniquity and the egregious sins of wearing these inferior crowns. Swallow up every word and deed that was done upon you. Swallow the innocent bloodshed, sexual sins, moving of the boundary stones, worship of ourselves, idol worship, occultic worship, theft...every sin under the sun that Jesus died for.

I charge you to swallow it up, and I bless you to your original design; I bless you to see the governing sons and to begin blessing us. Begin pouring out your riches of the abundance of the truth of life. I request the blood of Jesus to cover every place this was done upon you, in you. I speak to the frequencies of the wind to blow away the evil. To the water, to drown it, and to the fire to burn it. I speak to you to return to your original design, as the Lord created you and the earth. The earth is the Lord's and the fullness of it belongs to the Lord.

I speak peace and I thank You, Jesus. I thank the Just Judge. I thank You, Jesus, the author and the finisher of our faith. I commission the angels to render these righteous verdicts in the spirit and the natural.

I commission the angels to put this on record. Thank you, Just Judge, for honoring us and trusting us with the responsibility of wearing the Crown of Love and the Crown of Righteousness. Thank you for helping us occupy the territory you assigned us. I don't take this lightly and ask for supernatural assistance and help daily to govern well as Your sons, in the name of Jesus.

As a son, I call in the treasure that has been lost from the north, the south, the east, and the west in every age, realm, dimension, and time to fill the capacity of this section.

I am grateful to Heaven for revealing the red dragon, its inferior crowns, and its mission. I am grateful that Revelation tells us that this dragon has been pierced by God himself. Thank you for your kindness in helping us overcome the word of our testimony and the blood of the lamb.

I ask that all of this be done in time and out of time, and in every age, realm, and dimension, and that all of the spiritual debris, residue, and essences that were left behind by this inferior crown and the spirits that came with it be destroyed utterly. Thank You, Father, for what you did, Jesus, for giving us authority and dominion here.

Court Case for the Removal of the Crown of Antichrist Off of Someone

Father, I ask to step into the Mercy Court of Heaven on behalf of _____ to receive Mercy in our time of need. I request the accuser of the brethren be brought in as well as them and their entire generations and everyone related to them by blood, marriage, adoption, civil or religious covenant, from Your hand in the garden, and all the way forward as far as it needs to go, as well as my cloud of witnesses.

Your Honor, I agree with the adversary that they and their generations bowed their knees to this dragon, accepted the inferior crowns, and wore them proudly. I repent for the spirit of antichrist they bore and the inferior crown they took upon their heads. I repent for the pomp and circumstance, elitism, indoctrination, better-than-you attitude, and superiority complex we took on, as well as the indoctrination of others; I repent for embodying a false religion and for 'biting' those they were in stewardship over, releasing the poison. I repent for working with the false Crown of Delusion as well as the false Crown of Secrets. I repent for all of the secrets this inferior crown bore that they agreed with.

I repent for conspiring with the office, realm, and spirit of antichrist, for embodying it. I repent for participating in exploiting, polluting, and poisoning the church, the body, and the ecclesia. I repent for being a part of ending the lives of bodies of ecclesias, people, and churches. I repent for allowing, tolerating, being in league with, and cooperating with the Delilah spirit, Jezebel, and Ahab. We repent for opening an evil portal and for creating evil timelines for ourselves, our generations, and others. We repent for taking on this mantle, sitting on the seat, the throne, and in the office of antichrist and ruling unjustly over your people. I repent for seeking to be elevated to positions and seats of power or where they, who wore this inferior crown, elevated those who should not ever have been elevated. I repent for the pride and for lusting after power and greed.

I repent for the false clinging to the cross, the defilement and mockery of it, for seeking fame, being pretentious, full of pride, lofty, arrogant, and judging others. I repent for embodying false religion, for promoting and esteeming it. Forgive us and our generations for infiltrating the church, bringing this inferior crown and elevating others to it. Forgive us for leading others astray.

I request your blood, Jesus, the amendment of 'As If It Never Were', the destruction of the seat/office/throne, the closing of the portal, and the removal of the garments. Please remove its mantle, destroy the seat, and close the portal. I ask that you break the chains from those who have been impacted or who have agreed with those who have worn this inferior crown over the generations and those whom they were over. Please have these destroyed.

I request that the chains attached to us and our generations be cut, severed, destroyed, dismantled, and the ashes of them be brought to Jesus. I request a complete destruction, annulment, cancellation, and overturning of the office of the Crown of Antichrist, in the name of Jesus.

I also request that the angels clean up the spiritual debris, essences, and residues in time, out of time, and in every age, realm, and dimension to infinity. Burn it and give the ashes to Jesus.

I ask for Your righteous verdict or further counsel.

> [If further repentance is needed, follow the instructions of the court.]

With our righteous verdict in hand, I speak to the Earth. I speak to you that every one of our generations who stepped upon you, even those related to us by blood, marriage, adoption, civil or religious covenant. Earth, I have received a righteous verdict from the Courts of Heaven this day.

I bless you to hear the word of the Lord. I bless you to swallow up the iniquity and the egregious sins of wearing these inferior crowns. Swallow up every word and deed that was done upon you. Swallow the innocent bloodshed, sexual sins, moving of the boundary stones, worship of ourselves, idol worship, occultic worship, theft...every sin under the sun that Jesus died for.

I charge you to swallow it up, and I bless you to your original design; I bless you to see the governing sons and to begin blessing us. Begin pouring out your riches of the abundance of the truth of life. I request the blood of Jesus to cover every place this was done upon you, in you. I speak to the frequencies of the wind to blow away the evil. To the water, to drown it, and to the fire to burn it. I speak to you to return to your original design, as the Lord created you and the earth. The earth is the Lord's and the fullness of it belongs to the Lord.

I speak peace and I thank You, Jesus. I thank the Just Judge. I thank You, Jesus, the author and the finisher of our faith. I commission the angels to render these righteous verdicts in the spirit and the natural.

I commission the angels to put this on record. Thank you, Just Judge, for honoring us and trusting us with the responsibility of wearing the Crown of Love and Crown of Righteousness. Thank you for helping us occupy the territory you assigned us. I don't take this lightly and ask for supernatural assistance and help daily to govern well as Your sons, in the name of Jesus.

As a son, I call in the treasure that has been lost from the north, the south, the east, and the west in every age, realm, dimension, and time to fill the capacity of this section.

I are grateful to Heaven for revealing the red dragon, its inferior crowns, and its mission. I am grateful that Revelation tells us that God himself has pierced this dragon. Thank you for your kindness in helping us overcome the word of our testimony and the blood of the lamb.

I ask that all of this be done in time and out of time, and in every age, realm, and dimension, and that all of the spiritual debris, residue, and essences that were left behind by this inferior crown and the spirits that came with it be destroyed utterly. Thank You, Father, for what you did, Jesus, for giving us authority and dominion here.

Solutions

- Remove not only its mantle, the crown, and its seat, which is a throne, but also the Delilah's.
- Focus on the repentance work of those in the body of Christ who have been elevated to positions and seats of power. To those who have ruling and rank over the people, and to those who have tolerated Jezebel.
- Close the portal.
- Remove its garments.
- Request that the head of this snake be cut off from the rest.
- You must break off the chains of enslavement from this crown for the people.

———— ∞ ————

Chapter 12
The False Crown of Devouring

The seventh false crown is the *Crown of Devouring*. This head of the dragon is seeking whomever he may devour. He sniffs out the weak and those on the edge. He seeks whom he can devour. The dragon hunts after the sons to place this crown upon them. This is a fierce crown in league with the sons of perdition—the ones that have given themselves over to darkness, also referred to as Sons of Belial or S.O.B's.

Because sin leaves a stench, the dragon hunts you. He follows the trail of the stench of sin. If sin is in your life, he can smell you.

Jude 1:17-23:

> *17 But you, beloved, remember the words which were spoken before by the apostles of our Lord Jesus Christ: 18 how they told you that there would be **mockers** in the last time who would **walk according to their own ungodly lusts.***

*¹⁹ These are **sensual persons**, who **cause divisions, not having the Spirit**.*

*²⁰ But you, beloved, building yourselves up on your most holy faith, praying in the Holy Spirit, ²¹ keep yourselves in the love of God, looking for the mercy of our Lord Jesus Christ unto eternal life. ²² And on some have compassion, making a distinction; ²³ but others save with fear, pulling them out of the fire, **hating even the garment defiled by the flesh**. (Emphasis mine)*

Notice that Jude details some of their deeds:

- They mock
- They walk according to their own ungodly lusts
- They are sensual persons
- They cause divisions
- They walk in the wrong spirit

Some follow *darkness*, while others fall into it. There is a difference. This dragon hunts both. Most don't return when this crown is put upon their head. It's lethal. That's what devouring does.

With this crown, you lose all sensibility and sense of oneness.

The most hardened of hearts wear this crown.

This isn't just an atheistic view; this is <u>*a hatred of God*</u>, a turning away, and the true son of perdition. It's not like the average sinner wears this crown. This dragon *seeks to devour common sense* and commonalities in people's lives so *they cannot hear the voice of God or see God*. That is what this dragon seeks—to devour the truth. The darkest of the dark wear this crown.

To watch the news, you probably have said, "They have lost their minds!" That is what this devouring crown does. You lose all sense of reason. If you encounter someone with whom you cannot reason and who appears to lack common sense, this individual is likely under the influence of this crown.

It's not the average atheist or sinner who wears this crown. This is like the deepest, darkest, blackest-hearted people. The ones that consume babies and murder and are on a path of what we would call the evil ones. An example would be Adolf Hitler or some of his assistants. It is sniffing out sin. It works in tandem with all other crowns because *it seeks to devour*.

2 Thessalonians 2:3:

> *Let no one deceive you by any means; for that day will not come unless the falling away comes first, and the man of sin is revealed, the* **son of perdition**. *(Emphasis mine)*

John 17:12:

While I was with them in the world, I kept them in Your name. Those whom You gave Me I have kept; and none of them is lost except **the son of perdition,** *that the Scripture might be fulfilled. (Emphasis mine)*

There is no light in them.
There is only darkness.

Perdition typically refers to a state of perishing, being lost, dying, or destruction.

They have no light in them. The dragon seeks someone he can devour and take to hell with him.

When you sin,
it begins sniffing you out.

He roams about and seeks to devour things. He has been looking for the crowns he can claim. The other false crowns must be removed before addressing this one.

Atheists and those co-workers who don't believe they are wearing this crown, but they have purposefully stepped over into something really dark. *They have no conscience.*

Identifying the False Crown of Devouring

- Are they hiding secret sins?
- Are they heavily involved in darkness?
- Do their words express wickedness?
- Are they conniving?
- Do they have a hardened heart?
- Do they mock?
- Do they have sensibility?
- Do they have sense of oneness?
- Do they have a hard heart?
- Do they seek to devour common sense?
- Do they seek to devour commonalities in people's lives?
- Do they cause divisions?
- Do they despise the truth?
- Do they have no conscience?
- Are they filled with darkness?
- Have they stepped into a depth of darkness purposefully?

How Do These Characteristics Affect Businesses

What is outlined here is a profile of someone deeply compromised—someone whose heart, mind, and behavior have been shaped by darkness and deception. When individuals like this are placed in leadership roles or given influence within a business—especially a

Kingdom-oriented business—the consequences can be profoundly destructive, spiritually corrosive, and culturally toxic.

Let's break down how each of these traits can **negatively impact a business** and then tie it all together with some thoughts on how to safeguard against this kind of spiritual infiltration.

1. Are they hiding secret sins?

Impact: Secret sin invites spiritual darkness and deception. It creates a double life that erodes integrity and opens spiritual gateways to oppression, confusion, and eventual exposure. It sows seeds of mistrust in the team and blocks Heaven's favor.

2. Are they heavily involved in darkness?

Impact: Ongoing involvement with darkness—occult, witchcraft, perversion, abuse—brings spiritual contamination. It turns the business into a battleground of spiritual warfare. Even if success appears on the outside, **the foundation becomes compromised**, and judgment is inevitable unless addressed.

3. Do their words express wickedness?

Impact: Words shape the atmosphere. If someone speaks curses, mockery, lies, or manipulation, it defiles the environment. It brings fear, intimidation, and shame to those who hear, **killing creativity, trust, and peace.**

---

4. Are they conniving?

Impact: Deceitful individuals employ manipulation, strategy, and charm for their selfish ends. They deceive others for gain, turning a Kingdom business into a **political machine** rather than a spiritual mission. Betrayal and deception follow close behind.

---

5 & 9. Do they have a hardened (or hard) heart?

Impact: A hardened heart is closed to conviction, accountability, and compassion. It **resists the Holy Spirit** and deflects repentance. Such a leader is unteachable, defensive, and blind to their impact, creating a culture of control and callousness.

---

6. Do they mock?

Impact: Mockery is a weapon of pride and unbelief. It creates a hostile environment where spiritual things are not honored, and people are belittled. It often silences the prophetic voice and discourages boldness and authenticity in the workplace.

7. Do they have sensibility?

Impact: A lack of sensibility (moral perception and sound judgment) leads to rash decisions, missed spiritual cues, and unhealthy responses to conflict. The business lacks discernment and direction, becoming reactive rather than Spirit-led.

8. Do they have a sense of oneness?

Impact: Without a sense of oneness, there's no unity. The business becomes divided by personal agendas, competition, and disloyalty. It dismantles **team synergy and the commanded blessing** that comes with unity (Psalm 133).

10. Do they seek to devour common sense?

Impact: This points to **spiritual arrogance**, where practical wisdom is dismissed, and only their way or "revelation" is valid. It leads to dangerous decisions that ignore wise counsel, setting the business up for financial, legal, or relational ruin.

11. Do they seek to devour commonalities in people's lives?

Impact: This person isolates individuals by destroying unity, exploiting differences, and emphasizing division. It fosters a culture of suspicion, elitism, and cliques, rather than a shared vision and a Kingdom family.

---

12. Do they cause divisions?

Impact: Division is one of the most damaging spirits to a business. It fractures trust, splinters teams, and saps momentum. God doesn't bless disorder, and division opens the door for the enemy to disrupt purpose and vision.

---

13. Do they despise the truth?

Impact: If truth is rejected, lies are embraced. Such individuals manipulate narratives, conceal wrongdoing, and suppress criticism. The business becomes built on deception, and everything sacred is twisted for personal gain.

---

14. Do they have no conscience?

Impact: This is a clear indicator of **seared morality** and potential demonic influence. A conscienceless leader can justify abuse, theft, betrayal, and perversion without remorse. This is extremely dangerous and must be removed from influence.

15. Are they filled with darkness?

Impact: Darkness cannot partner with light. When someone filled with darkness is in authority, they **grieve the Holy Spirit, block revelation, and draw demonic influence.** Dreams, visions, and Kingdom impact are stifled.

16. Have they stepped into a depth of darkness purposefully?

Impact: This is not an accidental compromise; it's a willful rebellion. Such a person is a carrier of **spiritual death.** Their presence invites demonic strongholds and curses. Without repentance, they function as spiritual saboteurs within the business.

Final Thoughts:

When even one of these characteristics is present, especially in leadership, it **compromises spiritual safety, corrupts culture, and cuts off divine flow.** However, when several are active, the business may already be functioning under a counterfeit mantle, far from its original calling in the Kingdom.

Personal Court Case for the Removal of the Crown of Devouring

[Repentance for this crown needs to follow repentance for all the other false crowns.]

Father, I ask to step into Your Court of Mercy to receive mercy in our time of need. I ask that the accuser of the brethren be brought into this court as well as my generations, those related to me by blood, marriage, civil and religious covenant, all the way back to Your hand in the garden and all the way forward as far as it needs to go, and my cloud of witnesses.

Your Honor, this Crown of Devouring cannot be removed until the other crowns are removed. However, I would like to begin the court case process today.

Your Honor, I repent for myself and my generations for partnering, agreeing with, and participating with the darkest of the darkest of sins. I repent that I put myself and our generations in danger of being hunted because of these sins. I repent for our weaknesses in not seeking after God. I repent for our generations' sins that created a stench that the enemy could sniff out.

I repent for living on the edge, allowing this dragon to hunt us and those in our generations. I repent for being in league with the sons of perdition—the ones that have given themselves over to darkness. I repent for losing all sensibility and sense of oneness of our spirit, soul, and body in cooperation with the Lord. I repent for becoming and having the most hardened of hearts. I repent for having deliberately stepped into something dark and for agreeing to have no conscience.

I repent for allowing ourselves to be void of truth. I repent for taking up the other crowns and then wearing this one, the last. I repent for the lust of blood, the drinking of blood, and the eating of flesh from the kingdom of darkness. We are only to take in the blood and body of Christ. I repent for myself and our generations. I repent for the idea of getting near the unholy fire and letting it burn us and for basking in it, allowing it to consume us.

I request that all crowns be destroyed and that this specific crown be entirely removed and destroyed, as I have done the repentance work. I request the complete removal of this vile crown from our heads as well as from the heads of our generations. I ask that it be burned in the Holy Fire of the Lord God Almighty.

I request the amendment of 'As if it Never Were' and ask for restoration in the mighty name of Jesus.

Please burn the spiritual residue, essences, and debris. In Jesus' name, I ask for the Superior Crowns of the Kingdom of Heaven to be placed on our heads, overturning the egregiousness of our sins.

I ask for Your righteous verdict, your honor, or further counsel.

[If further counsel is advised, follow these instructions. Once you have received a righteous verdict, begin the following segment:]

I speak to the earth that every one of our generations who stepped upon you, even those related to us by blood, marriage, adoption, civil or religious covenant.

Earth, I have received a righteous verdict from the Courts of Heaven this day. I bless you to hear the word of the Lord. I bless you to swallow up the iniquity and the egregious sins of self-deception and wearing these crowns. Swallow up every word and deed that was done upon you. Swallow the innocent bloodshed, sexual sins, moving of the boundary stones, worship of ourselves, idol worship, occultic worship, theft…every sin under the sun that Jesus died for, as well as every evil covenant. I charge you to swallow it up and bless you to your original design. I bless you to see the governing sons and to begin blessing us. Begin pouring out your riches of abundance of truth and life.

I request the blood of Jesus to cover every place this was done upon you or in you. I speak to the frequencies of the wind to blow away the evil, to the water to drown it, and to the fire to burn it. I speak to you to return to your original design as the Lord had created you. The Earth is the Lord's, and its fullness belongs to the Lord.

I speak peace. I thank the Just Judge. I thank You, Jesus, the author and the finisher of our faith, for the Crowns of

Righteousness and the Crown of Love that trump this inferior crown.

As a governing son, I pick up these Superior Crowns, place them upon our heads, and ask you to help us rule. I commission the angels to render these righteous verdicts in the spirit and the natural. I commission the angels to put this on record.

Thank you, Just Judge, for honoring us and trusting us with the responsibility of wearing these Crowns of Love and Righteousness. Thank you for helping us occupy the territory you assigned us. I don't take this lightly and ask for supernatural assistance and help daily to govern well as Your sons, in the name of Jesus.

As a son, I call in the treasure that has been lost from the north, the south, the east, and the west in every age, realm, dimension, and time to fill the capacity of this section.

I ask that all of this be done in time and out of time, and in every age, realm, and dimension, and that all of the spiritual debris, residue, and essences that were left behind by this inferior crown and the spirits that came with it be destroyed utterly. Thank You, Father, for what you did, Jesus, for giving us authority and dominion here.

Court Case for the Removal of the Crown of Devouring Off Someone

[Repentance for this crown needs to follow repentance for all the other false crowns.]

Father, I ask to step into Your Court of Mercy on behalf of _____ to receive mercy in time of need. I ask that the accuser of the brethren be brought into this court as well as their generations, those related to them by blood, marriage, civil and religious covenant, all the way back to Your hand in the garden and all the way forward as far as it needs to go, and their cloud of witnesses.

Your Honor, this Crown of Devouring cannot be removed until the other false crowns are removed. However, I would like to begin the court case process today.

Your Honor, I repent for them and their generations for partnering, agreeing with, and participating with the darkest of the darkest of sins. I repent that they put themselves and their generations in danger of being hunted because of these sins. I repent for their weaknesses in not seeking after God. I repent for the sins of their generations that created a stench the enemy could sniff out.

I repent for them living on the edge, allowing this dragon to hunt them and those in their generations. I repent for them being in league with the sons of perdition—the ones that have given themselves over to darkness. I repent for them losing all sensibility and sense of oneness of our spirit, soul, and body in cooperation with the Lord. I repent for them becoming and having the most hardened of hearts. I repent for them having deliberately stepped into something dark and for agreeing to have no conscience.

I repent for allowing ourselves to be void of truth. I repent for them taking up the other crowns and then wearing this one. I repent for their lust of blood, for their drinking of blood, and the eating of flesh from the kingdom of darkness. We are only to take in the blood and body of Christ. I repent for them and their generations. I repent for the idea of getting near the unholy fire and letting it burn them and for basking in it, allowing it to consume them.

I request that all crowns be destroyed and that this specific crown be entirely removed and destroyed, as I have done the repentance work. I request the complete removal of this vile crown from our heads as well as from the heads of their generations. I ask that it be burned in the Holy Fire of the Lord God Almighty.

I request the amendment of 'As if it Never Were' and ask for restoration in the mighty name of Jesus.

Please burn the spiritual residue, essences, and debris. In Jesus' name, I ask for the Superior Crowns of the Kingdom of Heaven to be placed on their heads, overturning the egregiousness of their sins.

I ask for Your righteous verdict, Your Honor, or further counsel.

> [If further counsel is advised, follow these instructions. Once you have received a righteous verdict, begin the following segment:]

I speak to the earth that every one of their generations who stepped upon you, even those related to them by blood, marriage, adoption, civil or religious covenant.

Earth, I have received a righteous verdict from the Courts of Heaven this day. I bless you to hear the word of the Lord. I bless you to swallow up the iniquity and the egregious sins of self-deception and wearing these crowns. Swallow up every word and deed that was done upon you. Swallow the innocent bloodshed, sexual sins, moving of the boundary stones, worship of ourselves, idol worship, occultic worship, theft…every sin under the sun that Jesus died for. I charge you to swallow it up and bless you to your original design. I bless you to see the governing sons and to begin blessing us. Begin pouring out your riches of abundance of truth and life.

I request the blood of Jesus to cover every place this was done upon you or in you. I speak to the frequencies of the wind to blow away the evil, to the water to drown it, and to the fire to burn it. I speak to you to return to your original design as the Lord had created you. The Earth is the Lord's, and its fullness belongs to the Lord.

I speak peace. I thank the Just Judge. I thank You, Jesus, the author and the finisher of our faith, for the Crowns of Righteousness and the Crown of Love that trump this inferior crown.

As a governing son, I pick up these Superior Crowns, place them upon their heads, and ask you to help them rule. I commission the angels to render these righteous verdicts in the spirit and the natural. I commission the angels to put this on record.

Thank you, Just Judge, for honoring us and trusting us with the responsibility of wearing these Crowns of Love and Righteousness. Thank you for helping us occupy the territory you assigned us. I don't take this lightly and ask for supernatural assistance and help daily to govern well as Your sons, in the name of Jesus.

As a son, I call in the treasure that has been lost to them and their generations from the north, the south, the east, and the west in every age, realm, dimension, and time to fill the capacity of this section.

I ask that all of this be done in time and out of time, in every age, realm, and dimension, and that all the spiritual debris, residue, and essences left behind by this inferior crown and the spirits that accompanied it be utterly destroyed. I thank You, Father, for what you did, Jesus, for giving us authority and dominion here.

———— ∞ ————

Interaction of the Seven False Crowns

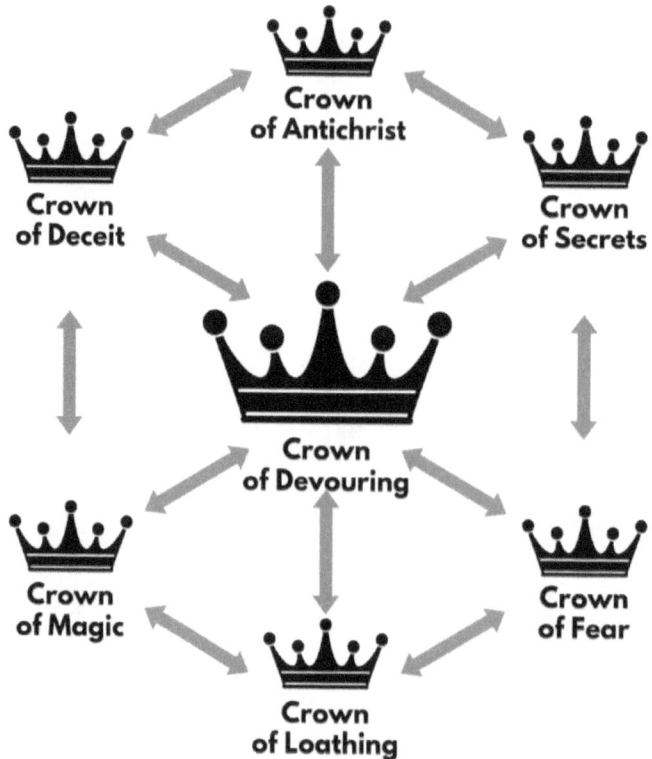

Copyright © 2025 LifeSpring Publishing

Chapter 13
Gaining Freedom From False Crowns

If you have worked through the court case for freedom from all seven of the false crowns, you may want to wrap up the court work in this manner:

Personal Court Work for Freedom from the Seven False Crowns

Father, I ask to step into Your Court of Crowns. I ask that the accuser of the brethren be brought into this court as well as my generations, those related to me by blood, marriage, civil and religious covenant, all the way back to Your hand in the garden and all the way forward as far as it needs to go.

I ask that the seven-headed dragon be brought in and muzzled and caged. I request that the accuser of the brethren and every Principality, power, demon, ruler of darkness, and evil entity that was associated with the seven-headed dragon, their inferior crowns, mantles, altars, thrones, and scepters, be brought in and gagged as well.

Having done repentance work for each of the seven crowns, Your Honor, I ask that the repentance work already accomplished and the verdicts be brought into evidence in this court this day. I also request our cloud of witnesses, the angels, and every witness to these events be brought into this court on our behalf.

I request that these seven heads be judged today, for they have inflicted pain, torment, anguish, and untold misery upon Your sons and daughters and the peoples of the earth. They have hindered the growth, abilities, expansion, and work of Your church on Earth. They have murdered, stolen, and destroyed without regard for You, Your sons, or Your purposes in the earth. They have laid evil and egregious crowns on the heads of Your sons to mock not only them but You.

I ask that each head be judged, cut off, and destroyed from our lives, and the damage be undone via the amendment of "As if it Never Were."

I ask that you please burn the inferior Crown of the Beast, which is set above the seven-headed dragon, the dragon, its seven heads, its inferior crowns, thrones, mantles, scepters, altars, spiritual residue, essences, and debris. In Jesus' name, I ask for the Superior Crowns of the

Kingdom of Heaven to be placed on our heads, overturning the egregiousness of our sins.

I ask for renewed authorization for every crown restored to us and those to be restored today in Your court.

I am grateful to Heaven for revealing the red dragon, its inferior crowns, associated evil entities, and its mission. I am grateful that Revelation tells us that this dragon has been pierced by God Himself. Thank You for your kindness in helping us overcome the word of our testimony and the blood of the lamb.

I ask that all of this be done in time and out of time, and in every age, realm, and dimension, and that all the spiritual debris, residue, and essences that were left behind by this inferior crown and the spirits that came with it be destroyed utterly. I also ask that these evil entities be judged in Your court this day, in Jesus' name.

I thank You, Father, for what you did, Jesus, for giving us the authority and dominion here.

Court Work for Freedom from the Seven False Crowns for Some Else

Father, I ask to step into Your Court of Crowns on behalf of _____. I ask that the accuser of the brethren be brought into this court as well as them and their generations, those related to us by blood, marriage, civil and religious covenant, all the way back to Your hand in the garden and all the way forward as far as it needs to go.

I ask that the seven-headed dragon be brought in and muzzled and caged. I request that the accuser of the brethren and every Principality, power, demon, ruler of darkness, and evil entity that was associated with the seven-headed dragon, their inferior crowns, mantles, altars, thrones, and scepters, be brought in and gagged as well.

Having done repentance work for each of the seven crowns, Your Honor, I ask that the repentance work already accomplished and the verdicts be brought into evidence in this court this day. I also request that they and their cloud of witnesses, the angels, and every witness to these events be brought into this court on their behalf.

I request that these seven heads be judged today, for they have inflicted pain, torment, anguish, and untold misery upon Your sons and daughters and the peoples of the earth. They have hindered the growth, abilities, expansion, and work of Your church on Earth. They have murdered, stolen, and destroyed without regard for You, Your sons, or Your purposes in the earth. They have laid evil and egregious crowns on the heads of Your sons to mock not only them but You.

I ask that each head be judged, cut off, and destroyed from our lives, and the damage be undone via the amendment of "As if it Never Were."

I ask that You please burn the inferior Crown of the Beast which is set above the seven-headed dragon, the dragon, its seven heads, its inferior crowns, thrones, mantles, scepters, altars, spiritual residue, essences, and debris. In Jesus' name, I ask for the Superior Crowns of the Kingdom of Heaven to be placed on our heads, overturning the egregiousness of our sins.

I ask for renewed authorization for every crown restored to us and those to be restored today in Your court.

I am grateful to Heaven for revealing the red dragon, its inferior crowns, associated evil entities, and its mission. I am grateful that Revelation tells us that this dragon has been pierced by God Himself. Thank You for Your kindness in helping us overcome the word of our testimony and the blood of the lamb.

I ask that all of this be done in time and out of time, in every age, realm, and dimension, and that all the spiritual debris, residue, and essences left behind by this inferior crown and the spirits that accompanied it be utterly destroyed. I also ask that these evil entities be judged in Your court this day, in the name of Jesus.

I thank You, Father, for what You did, Jesus, for giving us the authority and dominion here.

These seven false crowns are by no means the only ungodly crowns; they are simply seven primary categories of false crowns. These are the biggies. In your intercession, you will uncover and remove other ungodly crowns from these leaders. No matter what the crown's title, the great news is that the Superior Crowns of Heaven always trump it.

———— ∞ ————

Chapter 14
Superior Crowns

Any crown from Heaven is superior to the inferior crowns that Satan has devised or corrupted. We want the inferior false crowns replaced with the Superior Crowns of Heaven.

Where you find an inferior Crown of Strife, you want it removed and replaced with a Superior Crown of the Shalom of God. Where you find an inferior crown of division, you want it removed, the works of the crown destroyed, and place a Crown of the Unity of Heaven in its stead.

Crowns are critical for the sons to understand and for parents to understand and maximize in their own lives and the lives of their children. Authority in one's life can be reborn or reignited by the embrace of crowns. Some crowns come with a cost, while others are a result of the cost. The number of crowns available to the sons is immeasurable, for the Father wants our authority to be immeasurable.

> *The Father wants to see every inferior crown bowing to a Superior Crown.*

The sick man in Acts at the temple gate was wearing a Crown of Sickness, and it needed to be exchanged for a Crown of Wholeness.

When people carry a Crown of Depression or defeat, that inferior crown must bow to the Superior Crown of Hope and Victory. When you see how many are bent low under the weight of an inferior crown, see that inferior crown bowing to a Superior Crown. That is how the will of Heaven manifests. Replace the inferior crowns with Superior Crowns.

Remember, the Word says that in the name of Jesus, every knee will bow, and every tongue will confess the Lordship of Jesus.[7] That is an inferior crown bowing to the Superior Crown.

The Authority of Inferior Crowns

A principle of the Word is that all crowns carry a degree of authority related to the type of crown they

---

[7] Philippians 2:11

are. Therefore, if someone has received a Crown of Sickness, that crown will begin to manifest sickness of some sort in the person's body. As we learn to facilitate the exchange of inferior crowns with Superior Crowns, healing will manifest because a Crown of Wholeness carries with it the authority to release wholeness into a person, thereby defeating the operation of the Crown of Sickness.

> *Crowns are representative of the authority we carry in a particular arena.*

When you read authority-related verses, understand that the inferior is bowing to the superior. As the sons exercise the authority in the various crowns they carry, many who have been weighed down under the weight of inferior crowns will find those crowns coming off their heads and being replaced by a Superior Crown.

Every capability of the Father can be released and made resident in a crown. For healing, we have the expression of Jehovah Raphe (The Lord our Healer), for provision (Jehovah Jireh), for victory in battle, Jehovah Sabaoth (the Lord of Hosts), and more. His touch is in everything He has created. The crowns lack nothing.

> *You are responsible for the stewardship of the blessing contained in a particular crown.*

As you learn to walk and work *from the authority of a Superior Crown,* much will change. When you look in a mirror, see yourself carrying Superior Crowns.

In Luke 10:19, Jesus is speaking and says:

> Look, I have given you authority (of a Superior Crown) over **all** the power (inferior crowns) of the enemy, and you can walk among snakes and scorpions (operations of inferior crowns) and crush them. Nothing will injure you. (NLT) (Emphasis and additions mine)

Have you noticed that when we lay hands on someone to pray for them, we generally lay hands upon their head? We are essentially crowning them with whatever it is you are praying for them about or imparting to them. Parents, I suggest you draw your children close and begin to remove any inferior or false crowns you detect, replacing them with the Superior Crowns of Heaven. Teach your children to maintain their crowns by being aware of when the enemy tries to steal them. Also, teach them to access the Court of Crowns for themselves and gain the crowns Heaven wants for them.

These changes can apply to every area of your life. Parents, step into the Court of Crowns and receive what Heaven has for you, and receive the authority of the Superior Crowns. As sons, demonstrate a superior Kingdom. The time is now!

———— ∞ ————

Chapter 15
Strategies of Hell Against Crowns

It should not be a surprise to anyone that with the release of new revelations on crowns, hell has been trying to strategically work against this revelation. But first, Heaven wanted us to know that we can step into the Court of Crowns and receive *all* of the Godly crowns that Heaven has designed for us.

We need to repent for *not* picking up the crowns that we were due to have up to this point in our lives. Additionally, we need to repent for placing a false label on a crown. What do I mean by that?

Satan sometimes places false labels on crowns so that the crown is no longer desirable to us. He may imply that, "You don't want that crown, it's too hard," or "it will cost too much," or "It doesn't do what you think." He is simply nefarious like that. With the Crown of Knowledge, he was placing a false label on it (such as "heretic") so that we would not pick up that crown.

Instead, we need the angels of Heaven to remove every false label that has ever been placed on any of our crowns and request the strength of that crown to be restored in fullness.

The reason someone cannot detect the false label is that the veil over their spiritual eyes clouds their vision, and they cannot determine whether it is the crown's title or a false label on the crown. The image was of someone picking up a crown, trying it on, and then putting it down. They would keep only the ones they wanted, whereas we should want all the Kingdom of Heaven has for us.

Heaven wanted to unveil some of that to us, and in the engagement with Heaven, three books were presented before us. The first book was *Strategies of Hell: How the Enemy Uses Strategies Against Each Crown.*

The second book was *Removing the False Labels on Our Crowns.* We need to repent for the generations that picked up a crown from Heaven, only to see the false label placed upon it by the veil of the spirit of religion, which had been placed upon each of these Godly crowns.

Once we have repented, we need to step into the realms of Heaven and see all the Godly crowns available to the sons and recognize any false labels that the enemy has put upon these crowns: the label of heretic on some crowns, even those that were martyred. It was the crown that was labeled heretic, and the person had to endure much suffering. As sons, without the veil of religion hindering our sight, we can detect the false label and take those false labels off the Godly crowns. The cost has been paid. We don't have to consider the cost.

The third book was *Receiving Every Crown of Heaven Available to the Sons*. This book is about stepping into the Court of Crowns and receiving every crown of Heaven that is available to the sons. Also, to repent for the generations for picking up a crown that was from Heaven and seeing the false label from the veil of the spirit of religion that had been placed upon each of these Godly crowns, and rejecting that crown.

How do we deal with this?

1. Step into the realms of Heaven and into the Court of Crowns.
2. Acknowledge that we viewed the crowns with the label through the veil of the spirit of religion.
3. Repent.
4. Ask that the veil be removed so that we can see clearly.
5. Receive the crowns.

Court Scenario

As a son, I request access to the Court of Crowns.

I repent where I have viewed Heaven's crowns through the veil of religion. I come out of agreement with the spirit of religion and the veil it imposes upon my life. I want all of the crowns that you have available to us as your son.

I request that the false labels be removed.

I request that the false labels on every crown I picked up be removed from these crowns. I request reauthorization of the true purpose of this crown, along with all its aspects.

I also repent for our generations that embraced false labels and viewed crowns through the spirit of religion. I ask for your forgiveness. I ask that the veil be removed from my generations, and every false label removed.

I receive every crown you have intended for me and my generations with joy!

Thank you.

───── ∞ ─────

Chapter 16
Retrieving Lost Crowns

To maximize what Heaven provides through a crown, we need to understand those provisions. The typical components of a crown include:

- **The Crown** – The obvious representation of the authority you carry in the particular arena your crown encompasses.
- **The Mantle** – Coupled with the Anointing, this is the empowerment of Heaven for what your Crown represents and provides.
- **The Throne** – The seated place of your dominion.
- **The Anointing** that accompanies the crown. It is proof of the authorization of the Crown by Heaven.
- **The Scepter** – a secondary symbol of your Throne.
- **The Dominion** that the crown represents.

- **The Glory** – the expression of Heaven that you carry as you wear your crown.
- **The Resources** – the natural and supernatural things you will need to accomplish the mantle of a crown.

If Satan gets your crown he gets all the above.

If you drive on the highway and have a flat tire, you don't abandon the vehicle. You change the tire and continue to your destination. It's the same in our Christian walk. If we make a mistake, it's a temporary setback, not a permanent condition. So you messed up. Repent, get up, and go on. The enemy will say that you have disqualified yourself from all the Father has for you, which may be true as long as the setback is not repented. However, once it is repented of, move on. Don't even pause. Move forward without hesitation!

Setbacks that are unrepented of ***will*** diminish your authority, but once repented of, the authority is restored in full force. Recognize that the enemy uses those occasions to try to steal your crown. If it got knocked askew, repent, and place it firmly back on your head. Then, request the re-authorization of the authority of that crown.

Revelation 1:5:

May this grace and peace of Jesus Christ overwhelm you. He is the first born from the dead and embodies the evidence and testimony of everything that God believes about you. He heads up the authority in which we reign as kings on the earth. **His crown endorses our crown.** *He always loves us and loosed us once and for all from the dominion of sin in the shedding of his blood. (MIRROR) (Emphasis mine)*

Because Jesus wears His crown, you are fully qualified to wear your crown. He paid the price, he paved the way.

He bought your victory IN FULL at the resurrection.

The Mirror Translation says in Revelation 3:11:

Remember that <u>you</u> call the shots; <u>you</u> wear the crown. Don't let anyone steal your crown! (MIRROR) (Emphasis mine)

You choose to deal with the setbacks and move forward. Heaven isn't stopping you, and hell CANNOT stop you! Only *you* can stop you.

WEAR YOUR CROWN!

If you find these things difficult, it may be that Satan has already stolen some crowns from you. The following is a list of Business-Related Crowns we have identified. It is by no means complete. These may be crowns you have lost or crowns you need to gain. Access your Book of Crowns from the Court of Crowns and begin the process. Directions on the process are in this chapter.

Business-Related Crowns

- Crown of Abundance
- Crown of Administration
- Crown of Affluence
- Crown of Authority
- Crown of Blessing
- Crown of Blessings of the Lord
- Crown of Business
- Crown of Business Acumen
- Crown of Business Intelligence
- Crown of Business Strategy
- Crown of the Captain of Industry
- Crown of Clarity
- Crown of Commerce
- Crown of Courage
- Crown of Deuteronomy 28:1-14
- Crown of Discernment
- Crown of Elevation
- Crown of Economy
- Crown of Faithfulness

- Crown of Favor
- Crown of Finance
- Crown of Financial Commerce
- Crown of Freedom
- Crown of Fruitfulness
- Crown of Glory
- Crown of Health
- Crown of Identity
- Crown of Increased Territory
- Crown of Industry
- Crown of Influence
- Crown of Inheritance
- Crown of Joy
- Crown of Keys
- Crown of Kingship
- Crown of Kingdom Expansion
- Crown of Laughter as Medicine
- Crown of Life
- Crown of Might
- Crown of Multiplication
- Crown of Networking
- Crown of Occupying
- Crown of Ownership
- Crown of Pearls
- Crown of Prosperity
- Crown of Sanctification
- Crown of Sonship
- Crown of Spheres of Influence)
- Crown of Stability
- Crown of Stars

- Crown of Steadiness
- Crown of Stewardship
- Crown of Success
- Crown of the Anointing for Business
- Crown of the Blessings of Father Abraham
- Crown of Trade
- Crown of Understanding
- Crown of Wealth Transfer
- Crown of Wisdom
- Crown of Witty Inventions

Business owners, be aware that the enemy will attempt to send people across your path, as well as that of your team members and clients or customers, whose job is to steal crowns. Be aware of that strategy. These spoilers can do significant damage.

As a team member, if you are aware of your spiritual role, be diligent about assisting the owner in interceding for those on the team. The greater the unity within the business, the greater its impact on the marketplace.

Where we contributed to the loss or forfeiture, we must repent and then go to the Court of Crowns to receive renewed authorization for the authority that had been lost. Request that of the court, having repented for losing that crown. Then, commission the angels to begin bringing in what has been lost and fill the capacity. That capacity can also be enlarged. Let's get them back!

Stephanie prayed:

I request access to the Court of Crowns.

Your Honor, where I laid down my authority, or my generations did, and stepped out of our authority, I want to acknowledge that and take responsibility for it. I repent of it and ask that the authority and territory taken be re-established in the name of Jesus.

Where others were involved in the loss or theft of our crowns, I forgive them, bless them, and release them. I ask for the restoration of the crowns.

I ask this court for renewed authorization of the authority that was lost due to the forfeiture or loss of our crown(s).

I also thank the court for the establishment and the capacity of the promised land that have not been able to come forth because of us not governing correctly as sons, but I now understand the capacity of what I am and whose I am as I indeed take in the territory, the lands, the inheritances, and all that has been established here in the name of Jesus.

I commission the angels to bring these things from this place into the natural realm on behalf of the sons, so that I might be a good steward of what you give me.

As Stephanie prayed, she gained a bird's-eye view of the Court of Crowns and realized they were inside a crown.

Retrieval of Lost, Forfeited, or Stolen Crowns

You need to determine if Satan has stolen crowns from you and those in your business. How? Simply ask, "Has Satan stolen crowns from me/my spouse/my children?"

The answer should be simple to determine. "Yes, or no?" If yes, which I'm sure it will be, then begin to specify various crowns that you feel were taken from you. You could also do this from within the Court of Crowns by observing your personal *Book of Crowns*. You may also find you have crowns displayed in the Trophy Room of Hell.

Once you have a sense of what you have lost due to his thievery, here are the steps of retrieval:

1. Access the Court of Crowns.
2. Repent for our part in the loss of the crown(s)
3. Request the restoration of those crowns you lost.
4. Commission angels to retrieve the crowns from the trophy room of hell and bring them to you.
5. Take them from the angels.
6. Put them on your head.
7. Request the re-authorization of those crowns upon your life.
8. Commission angels to retrieve what was lost or stolen from you, from the north, south, east, west, and every age, realm, and dimension.

Finally, we must understand that a continual association with the victory Jesus purchased for us is necessary to maintain your crown(s).

Revelation 3:12:

> *It is in your individual,* **continual association with your[8] victory in me** *that I will make you to be like a strong pillar in the inner shrine of God's sanctuary, supporting the entire structure of my God-habitation within you. A place to be your permanent abode from whence you will never have to depart. And I will engrave upon you the name of my God, also the name of the city [the bride] of my God, the new Jerusalem that descends from heaven; as well as my own new Name. (MIRROR) (Emphasis mine)*

———— ∞ ————

---

[8] A continual, habitual victory

Chapter 17
The Crown of Communion

Our engagement on this day was shortly before Passover, and Heaven was preparing to celebrate. As Passover and Resurrection Day approach, the celebrations intensify. As we sat down at the table before us in the Library of Revelation, crowns were at each seat. Stephanie saw a series of images flashing before her eyes rapidly.

The scene kept changing from her family to her friends and others she would want to invite to sit at the table with us. She understood that the crowns in front of us were the Crowns of Communion for each of us.

She began to realize that this communion is broader than what we take as literal communion with bread and wine, but it is a picture of communion with one another. The Father's plan all along was communion with Him and with one another. Unity of family, not just blood relatives, but family, friends, and community. This has been the original design.

As she observed, Stephanie saw different people sitting at the same table. The people would shift from one group to another in an instant. This was the Father's original design.' Communion is an imperative part of *our* design as individuals. John the Revelator had joined us, and he picked up the Crown of Communion on the table in front of him and placed it on his head. He explained that Communion with family and close friends had become a disaster, and the Father seeks to restore communion within the Body of Christ. He sets a time to recognize and honor the body and blood of Jesus, as it is imperative. This communion is with and for each other within the Body. The Body has been deeply divided and broken, beginning with and through the spirit of religion, bringing division, offense, carelessness, accusations, sin, and iniquity. Father's desire is for the sons to walk in communion with one another.

John explained that receiving and wearing the Crown of Communion would help heal the divides because the community of the Body of Christ is broken, and the Father is beginning *reparations* for community, communion, faith, hope, and love in and between family. He encouraged us to take our crown. Understand that the Lord has already been preparing your family, and because He loves, it will abound.

Take time, this Passover season, and reflect upon His death, burial, and resurrection, and be mindful of the Crown of Communion. Remember the price that He paid once and for all, as His heart's desire is community and family, *and* He's longing for the original design to be brought into the hearts of men. Seek the Kingdom of God and His righteousness first, and all of these things shall be added unto you. This body of believers (Sandhills Ecclesia, LifeSpring) has sought the Kingdom of God and His righteousness. Boldly take the Crown of Communion and remember.

John exited, and someone else came and sat at the table that Stephanie did not immediately recognize. They reached over and took her by the arm. It was a young man. Still not realizing who it was, she looked deeper and discovered it was her son, the one she had aborted many years prior. She had seen him in Heaven on previous occasions, but never at the age she perceived him that day. She was joyfully taken aback.

He said, "I am being restored to you through Communion." She began to realize she could have communion with those in Heaven when she stepped into Heaven, she could call their spirits forth, just as we sometimes do when conducting court cases. We can have them sit down with us and share communion.

I suggested, "He may have a strategy for your daughters and your new son-in-law." A friend engaged with Heaven, and her father met with her, giving her prayer strategies for her sons.

As she sat with her son, she realized that she had taken away from him the relationships he would have had with his sisters and with his mother, grandmother, and father. All these relationships had been torn from him due to the abortion.

Her son said, "You can bring their spirits here. Those who have lost loved ones can find communion here at the table. It's a table prepared in the presence of your enemies. Restoration and communion do make the enemy angry.

As he said the last phrase, Stephanie noticed, through what seemed to be a window from another dimension, that the enemy was watching her conversation with her son. He was fuming with anger. As it says in Psalm 23:5:

You prepare a table before me in the presence of my enemies; You anoint my head with oil; my cup runs over.

Her son added, "Mom, it wasn't until you took the Crown of Communion that you could see this. Help others to know. Help others to see that, Mom."

He continued, "To be able to walk into the realms of Heaven, to have communion and community here, in Heaven, is the real deal. It's greater than anything you could think or imagine, the way and manner that you can come here and experience it."

Stephanie remarked, "I want that. I know that when I call the spirits of my children and my mother into Heaven, I will bless them and put the armor of God on them. I know that my son is going to have communion with them and that all of us who have loved ones in Heaven can come to the table. I can't wait to tell them this. Thank you, son."

Now, pause, request access to the Court of Crowns, and receive your Crown of Communion. You may want to call someone you love to sit with you in Heaven at the table and share communion. It is life-changing!

Those you call the spirits of into Heaven don't have to be told what you are doing. Their spirit will know, even though their soul may be puzzled. Wait for the testimonies that will eventually come forth from this "dream (or daydream) I had" or something similar. Enjoy the communion.

―――― ∞ ――――

Chapter 18
Helpful Assistance

No doubt, you could read through the lists of questions under the category of Identifying the False Crowns and identify crowns on those in your business. However, we don't just need to look at the employees; we need to look at every major contributor to the company. Some prayers and court work will also be required for other influencers in the lives of your team members.

For example, you want your team members surrounded by Godly friends and confidants. We want those advisors to provide wise, Godly counsel. We want our business shielded from those who would give wicked or worldly counsel.

Prophetic Intercessors

We need prophets who can advise our business of strategies against us such as what happened in 2 Kings 6:8-12:

> *⁸ Once when the king of Syria was warring against Israel, he took counsel with his servants, saying, 'At such and such a place shall be my camp.'*
>
> *⁹ But the man of God sent word to the king of Israel, 'Beware that you do not pass this place, for the Syrians are going down there.' ¹⁰ And the king of Israel sent to the place about which the man of God told him. Thus he used to warn him, so that he saved himself there more than once or twice. ¹¹ And the mind of the king of Syria was greatly troubled because of this thing, and he called his servants and said to them, 'Will you not show me who of us is for the king of Israel?'*
>
> *¹² And one of his servants said, 'None, my lord, O king; but* **Elisha, the prophet who is in Israel, tells the king of Israel the words that you speak in your bedroom.'** *(Emphasis mine)*

May these men and women with no agenda other than serving the Father faithfully arise and assist your business.

Angelic Forces

As we pray for our business team, we want the angels of Heaven involved. We want their personal angels on duty, and our business angels alert and on duty. We want them patrolling their bridges and gates and helping them fulfill their scroll.

Hopefully, your business team is surrounded by a Godly support system of Godly men and women.

As we perform this intercession, we will need to activate the angels of our coworkers, supervisors, mentors, and others, and commission these angels to accomplish the will of the Father. Additionally, we will have each person's scroll read to them regularly by the angels.

You may need to activate them for the team member you are praying for, who may have no concept of angels or of co-laboring with their angels. You can help their angels get activated and duly commissioned. Those who have experienced divorce also need the angels of their exes activated so they can help the ex cooperate with what Heaven is doing.

Realize that some of your team members may have angels who need respite. Request backup angels to be assigned until the primary angels are recovered enough to return to duty.

Occasionally, you may need to request replacements for their angels from the Court of Angels, as some may not be able to fulfill their duties sufficiently. If you notice, in your intercessions, someone who has constant assaults, and their angels always seem to be bested by the attacks, they either need additional help or replacement, or both. Utilizing their angels to assist in the work is invaluable. This is a rare occurrence, but it is essential to be aware of the possibility.

Additionally, you want your angels to collaborate with the angels assigned to your customers, vendors, or suppliers. One of the best ways to co-labor with these angels is to pray in the spirit for them. That will help them by providing the direction of Heaven for them.

You may want to find out the name of some of these angels so you can co-labor with them in a more targeted fashion.

These angels are ready to fulfill the Word of the Lord. Many times, they are simply awaiting instructions from the saints. Not every instruction for angels comes directly from Heaven. Some instructions come through the sons who know how to cooperate with Heaven and with the Angels.

Patrollers

Patrollers are men and women in white who roam geographical areas like scouts, observing the activities in those areas to deliver information to the saints. You can read about some in Zechariah 1. You can engage the patrollers in specific areas to gather intelligence on events that require the angels to be released or intercession in a particular area. I have more information in my book *Engaging the Courts for Your City*.[9] Some of these patrollers can also help you be aware of traps set for your co-workers, so you can take care of those traps and tricks of the enemy.

Watchers

Additionally, Heaven has watchers (angels who oversee a region's landscape) assigned to aid in the work. Most teaching about watchers is focused on evil watchers. They both perform similar functions, one for the Kingdom of God and the other for Satan.

These Godly watchers can also be consulted for intelligence about the enemy's plans in a particular area or against your coworkers. Don't overlook them. Co-labor with them.

Role Models

Having Godly role models for businesses is quite beneficial. You and your leadership team need them as

---

[9] *Engaging the Courts for Your City* by Dr. Ron M. Horner. LifeSpring Publishing (2019).

do your employees. Ask Heaven to provide some Godly role models for your team members.

Some readers of this book have been able to effectively help their business team with their crowns and with angelic commissioning. You may consider assisting other businesses around you with these concepts by providing a role model for them and their team members.

———— ∞ ————

Chapter 19
Fruit Inspectors

As you look at the societal landscape, some businesses have given themselves wholly over to many of the false crowns we discussed earlier. It is not our aim to judge them, but it is apparent what crowns some are wearing, and it is imperative that we, as sons, know how to intercede for them effectively.

Matthew 12:33:

Either make the tree good and its fruit good, or else make the tree bad and its fruit bad; for a tree is known by its fruit.

The question to ask is, "Whom do we start with?" Ask for the strategy of Heaven. Access the Court of Strategy and request that strategies be unlocked. Who do you pray for and how? Once you know who or what your intercession's focus should be, begin identifying what false crowns they are wearing that need to be replaced with Superior Crowns. Part of this process will be calling them back to where they should be as sons. Their sin has caused them to miss the mark and forfeit the prize.

They have received a Crown of Authority, as have we all, but what is that crown filled with? Does it have an overflow of the Glory of God, or is it filled with the vileness of hell? Some have made ungodly trades or other factors to get where they are. We must separate the man or woman from their deeds. We need to see who they really are. If you don't love them, however, stop praying for them. You will pray incorrectly for them. Ask the Father for a love for them. Ask Him to help you see them as He sees them. You may perform some acts of kindness on their behalf.

Jude had this counsel for us to consider in Jude 1:17-23:

> *17 But you, beloved, remember the words which were spoken before by the apostles of our Lord Jesus Christ: 18 how they told you that there would be mockers in the last time who would walk according to their own ungodly lusts.*
>
> *19 These are sensual persons, who cause divisions, not having the Spirit.*
>
> *20 But you, beloved, building yourselves up on your most holy faith, praying in the Holy Spirit, 21* **keep yourselves in the love of God,** *looking for the mercy of our Lord Jesus Christ unto eternal life. 22 And* **on some have compassion,**

making a distinction; [23] *but others save with fear, pulling them out of the fire, hating even the garment defiled by the flesh.* (Emphasis mine)

Those opting for false and inferior crowns haven't been introduced to the goodness of the Father. They don't know Him like you do...yet.

Understanding the significant influences our team members face by recognizing false crowns will help us remove those false crowns. We want them replaced with Godly crowns. We also want to see their Crown of Authority filled with the Glory of Heaven rather than the vileness that some are filled with now. Don't forget to place the Crown of Everlasting upon their heads to help awaken them to the goodness of the Father.

We want to see the change mentioned in Malachi 4:6 modeled in our families:

And he will turn the hearts of the fathers to the children, and the hearts of the children to their fathers.

Although everyone has a Crown of Authority, many have their crown filled with the wrong substance. We want our crowns to be filled with the Glory and substance of the Father. When we see someone, whose crown is contaminated by darkness, we can repent on their behalf, forgive their sins, and request their crown be cleansed and filled with the Glory of Heaven.

When we see someone wearing a Crown of Loathing, we can repent on their behalf, forgive them their sins, request the wrap-around love of God be poured into their lives, and the Crown of Loathing be replaced with a Crown of Grace and a Crown of the Love of the Father.

Those wearing a Crown of Fear, like those with a Crown of Loathing, need it replaced with a Crown of the Wrap-around Love of the Father. Apply these patterns to those wearing the false crowns of the seven-headed dragon, so that they may experience the love and might of God in their lives.

---

*People don't serve God
because they don't know God.
To know Him is to love Him.*

---

*The work of intercession is to align
a company's team members
with Heaven's purposes.*

Over the last several years, forces have been at work to destroy Christian companies. It's time for the sons to arise, step into their governing role, and legislate from the Courts of Heaven the purposes of God for our country and the families within our country.

When we, through the perception of our spirit, look at our leadership team, employees, contractors, or others, ask what the Father has for them. Regardless of what their crowns are filled with, the Father has a plan for them. Some are precisely where they are supposed to be. Others have been taken off course. May our intercession create a course correction in their life so they can fulfill God's purposes.

———— ∞ ————

Chapter 20
Entities & Their Crowns

We had already completed this book (or so we thought) when, in our engagement with Heaven, we learned that any entity established by Heaven has at least one crown. Once we discovered the content of this chapter, we inserted it, realizing that it might take another book to unpack what we need to know about entities and crowns.

Entities are living beings. They are sentient. They have life and can grow and expand. Entities also have stars that function under the title of the Bright and Morning Star. This engagement was again going to broaden our understanding of crowns. Particularly when we heard Malcolm say, "**Crowns don't just belong on people, they belong on entities from Heaven**. Isn't it about bringing the Kingdom of Heaven to earth?

During the engagement, Malcolm presented us with the LifeSpring Outstanding Folder, which is typically used to identify outstanding items that we need to address when working with the realms of Heaven. As he spoke, he tossed small crowns into our Outstanding Folder. He explained that everything brought from Heaven onto and into the earth has an eternal order or orbit. We must think bigger. Heaven's destiny and thrones are not just for the sons; therefore, His Kingdom principles. LifeSpring is a Kingdom ordinance and principle from the Kingdom of Heaven brought to the earth through the sons.

Malcolm then instructed us to bring LifeSpring into its orbit and crown it.

"Are you not governing sons?" he asked.

Asking him how we would bring them into its orbit, he said to order it as a governing son.

Stephanie asked, "How do we bring LifeSpring into its order so that we can crown it?" She also had a second question, "What crowns are for the entity that is LifeSpring?"

Malcolm replied, "Now you're asking the right questions."

A prayer welled up within Stephanie:

Father, we ask that LifeSpring International Ministries— the entity of it, its order and its orbit, be brought under the Bright and Morning Star, that the entity that is LifeSpring be crowned with the Crown of His Glory (as we sit under that order), and that all the crowns from the

Kingdom of Heaven, its strategies, it's plans purposes, destinies, maps, scrolls, and blueprints fill this crown and the order thereof.

Malcolm instructed, "Now bring into order: the Help Desk, the Outstanding Folder, the Bond Registry, and then the sons (who are part of LifeSpring).

Stephanie declared,

We bring this into order under the Crown of His Glory that sits under the Bright and Morning Star.

Stephanie saw a picture of the Bright and Morning Star with LifeSpring underneath it, and the Help Desk, the Outstanding Folder, the Bond Registry, and then the sons coming into alignment underneath it. It's as if I'm looking at an organizational chart. What Stephanie did not know was that less than two hours before, I had been talking with a colleague in our Heaven Down Business division, who shared that Heaven had unpacked the same information to them that morning. Our engagement confirmed the earlier information and vice versa. We were thrilled to have such rapid confirmation of a revelation.

We ask to step into the Court of Crowns. We present to you this organizational chart and the crown thereof of the Crown of His Glory and all other crowns that need to be put onto the entity of LifeSpring and all the components of it that include Heaven Down Business, Sandhill Ecclesia, AfterCare, LifeSpring School of

Ministry, the LifeSpring South Africa School, CoursNet...everything involved.

We were reminded that alignment helps things flow more smoothly, and Heaven helped us understand how the components of LifeSpring are meant to align. In all the revelations about crowns, I had not yet understood that entities also have crowns. These crowns designate authority in some manner. He also reminded us to be sure that no one removes our crown from us. We had experienced that not too long ago, when concerted efforts were made to steal my crowns and those of others in leadership at LifeSpring. They were unsuccessful, and immediately following those attempts, the revelation of the crowns began to unfold for us.

Some had also tried to defile the mantle we carry concerning revelation. During this encounter, Malcolm removed the fingerprints of those who had sought to take my mantle. We are grateful for what Malcolm did on our behalf.

We, again, asked permission to step into the Court of Crowns, where Stephanie prayed:

We ask to step into the Court of Crowns. We present to you this organizational chart and the crown thereof of the Crown of His Glory and all other crowns that need to be put onto the entity of LifeSpring and all the components of it that include Heaven Down Business, Sandhill Ecclesia, AfterCare, LifeSpring School of

Ministry, the South African School, CourtsNet... everything involved.

We had seen three nine-foot-long tables earlier, so we began to discern what was on each table. First, however, we knew the numbers 3, 9, and 27 were significant, so I did a little digging. Three refers to completeness and order. Nine marks the end of a cycle. It indicates the conclusion of a process or the finalization of a judgment. The number twenty-seven equals 3 X 3 X 3 or (3^3). When you cube it you have a sense of multiplied spiritual perfection or Heaven's signature deepened. It can represent the fullness of spiritual authority, divine completion, and heavenly expression—not just in one area, but in every dimension (like width, depth, height) as found in Ephesians 3:18-19:

> *...that you may be able to comprehend...what is the width and length and depth and height—to know the love of Christ...*

The number 27 is the depth of understanding divine mysteries. The New Testament contains 27 books. These 27 books represent grace, sonship, and Kingdom life. It also speaks to the integration of character and power, not one or the other, but both working together in full harmony.

You are not just gifted, you are formed. You don't just move in power—you carry the nature of the Father. In early Jewish thought, 27 represented light revealed.

More associations can be made. The 3, 9, and 27 were certainly not accidental.

First Table

Stephanie requested the names of the crowns we would place upon LifeSpring. A Crown of Honor was the first, then a Crown of Integrity, and finally a Crown of Friendship. These crowns were all in a row. In the next row, there was a bigger crown, the Crown of Sonship (different from the Crown of Sonship we learned about much earlier). This crown was awarded to those who had connected with LifeSpring and were embracing and growing in sonship through their relationship with LifeSpring. As they grasp this revelation, they receive the Crown of Sonship and gain an understanding of it.

The third set of crowns on the first table consisted of five: a Crown of Engagement, a Crown of Revelation, a Crown of Wisdom, a Crown of Understanding, and a Crown of Seek Ye First the Kingdom of God. The next crown has two crowns with it, a Crown of Singularity (regarding the uniqueness of this ministry and its set apartness). With the Crown of Singularity was the Crown of Strength. The last crown on this table was the Crown of Union.

Second Table

On the second table, we saw one singular crown on the first row—the Crown of Purpose. The second row had two crowns: a Crown of Dividing the Truth (we are supposed to divide the truth rightly) and a Crown of Truth. The third row had three crowns: a Crown of War (we are warring by wearing this crown, as we are warring from Heaven). The second crown that was with it was the Crown of the Horses of Heaven. It was like a stampede and a movement of the spirit. It's a good crown. Remember when Elijah was taken up in the chariot and Elisha called out, "The Chariots of Israel and its Horsemen". This seemed to be the essence of this crown. The third crown was the Crown of Fire. On the next row was a singular crown, the Crown of Stewardship.

The next row contained two crowns stacked one on top of the other. The Crown of Financial Gain is the top one, and the Crown of the Vault is the one below that.

On the next row was a singular crown: the Crown of Stretching.

Third Table

Moving to the third table was a huge crown—the Crown of the King. It took up the entire table. As Stephanie looked inside this crown, she saw within it the Crown of the Priest, the Crown of the Sword, and the Crown of the Spirit.

She prayed:

We request that they be established and placed on the entity known as LifeSpring and all its components in order, which is also an orbit. We thank you for the order, the orbit, and the establishment of the Kingdom. We're requesting authorization for these crowns, and I'm asking that special forces angels be assigned to guard them to prevent them from being knocked off, stolen, or given away.

As she prayed, she could feel them resting upon her head. She continued:

In the mighty name of Jesus, we honor the King and the Kingdom.

We thank you for the keys, scrolls, maps, portals, and doorways. Doorways is one of the words I heard that are being opened as the windows of Heaven are being opened.

We commission and ask for the angels assigned to all of these crowns we have been given, the Crown of Stewardship to steward this wealth on behalf of the Kingdom of Heaven, for the sons, for the sake of the Earth. We glorify you, Lord.

We request authorization for these crowns to be given to the sons. We thank you that the Earth and the fullness thereof belong to the Lord. May we be good stewards.

Malcolm walked over to the whiteboard, took the Outstanding Folder from where it had been attached, and said, "It's like all of it's in order now," and he walked away.

It may take some time to unpack the revelation of the different crowns, but we intend to fully cooperate with every aspect of these crowns as we endeavor to expand the Kingdom of Heaven on the earth.

You will want to engage Heaven and the Court of Crowns to discover the crowns Heaven has in mind for your business. The resources of Heaven are limitless to the sons! Happy Hunting!

Chapter 21

Epilogue

Many believers have lost the strength that comes with the crowns they once possessed. I discussed how to regain lost, forfeited, or stolen crowns. This book was about embracing the crown's understanding on behalf of your business and maximizing these crowns. Since the focus of this book has been business intercession, we must know the answer to the following question:

How do we apply the understanding of crowns and business intercession?

As we have received the full activation of our Crown of Authority and our Crown of Kingdom Expansion, these will provide the resources to begin the work:

1. Ask Heaven for greater love for those you are praying for.
2. Gain access to the Court of Crowns.
3. Ask for the strategy of Heaven.

4. Identify the false crowns at work in the lives of those in your business.
5. Begin the repentance work (use the various Court Scenarios provided in this book).
6. Get the false and ungodly crowns removed from them.
7. Petition Heaven on their behalf for the Superior Crowns of Heaven for them.
8. Get them placed upon their heads.
9. Go to the next person and continue the process.

Once you have completed this for your business, begin this work on behalf of the influencers in your business, whether they are extended team members, former employees, or others. Keep tabs on the progress made within your business so that they can all maximize what Heaven wants to do.

May your business and those who benefit from it experience the riches of Heaven provided through the crowns.

———— ∞ ————

Appendix

Learning to Live Spirit First

A challenge with how we were taught about the Christian life is that everything was put off until sometime in the future. Then, we read Paul's letters and experienced a disconnect. Heaven, to us, was a destination, not a resource. We knew nothing about learning to live from our spirits. We only knew what we had been doing since birth, and that was to live to satisfy our soul or flesh. We sorely need to learn an alternative way of living.

Exchanging Our Way of Living

Paul recorded these words in his letter to the Romans:

Romans 8:5:

> *Those who are motivated by the flesh only pursue what benefits themselves. But those who live by the impulses of the Holy Spirit are motivated to pursue spiritual realities.*

We must learn to live spirit first! We must exchange our way of living. We must learn to live from our spirit. We need to understand the hierarchy within us:

a. We are a spirit.
b. We possess a soul.
c. We live in a body.

Each component has a specific purpose in our lives. Our spirit is the interface with the supernatural realm. It is designed for interfacing with Heaven and the Kingdom realm. Our spirit has been in existence in our body since conception. Our soul has a different purpose. It communicates to our intellect and our physical body what our spirit has obtained from Heaven. It is the interface with our body. Our body houses the two components and follows the dictates of whichever component is dominating,

Most of us have never been taught about having our spirit dominate. Rather, we have merely assumed that our soul being dominant was the required mode of operation.

Our soul always wants to be in charge. Our soul is susceptible to carnal or fleshly desires, lusts, and behaviors. It will, at times, resist our spirit and body. It must be made to submit to our spirit by an act of our will.

Our will is a means of instructing either component (spirit, soul, or body) in what to do. Our soul has a will, and so does our spirit. We choose who dominates!

Our body, on the other hand, has appetites that will control us in subjection to our soul. They become partners in crime—remember that second piece of chocolate cake it wanted? Our body will try, along with our soul, to dictate our behavior. It will likely resist the spirit's domination of our lives. However, it will obey our spirit's domination if instructed, and our body can aid our spirit if trained to do so.

The typical expression that operates in most people's lives is that their soul is first, body second, and their spirit is somewhere in the distance in last place.

In some people, especially those very conscious of their physical fitness or physical appearance, there is a different lineup. Their body is their priority, the soul second, and again, their spirit is the lowest priority.

Heaven's desire for us is vastly different. Heaven desires that we live spirit first, soul second, and body third. Since we are spiritual beings, this is the optimal arrangement. For most of us, our spirit was not activated in our lives in any measure until we became born again.

If, after our salvation experience, we began to pursue our relationship with the Father, then we became much more aware of our spirit and learned to live more spirit-conscious. The apostle Paul wrote in his various epistles about living in the spirit or walking in the spirit.

> *Because we are spiritual beings, our spirits cry out for a deepening of relationship with the Father.*

Our spirit longs for it and will try to steer us in that direction. Many of us had a hunger for God from early in our lives.

Our soul has certain characteristics that explain its behavior in our life. This is the briefest of lists, but I think we will get the idea. Our soul is selfish. It wants what it wants when it wants it. It can be very pouty. It can act like a small child. It is offendable and often even looks for opportunities to be offended. Our soul is also rude.

Our body has a different set of characteristics. It is inconsiderate, demanding, lazy, and self-serving. It does not want to get out of bed in the morning, for many people. In others, it wants to be fed things that are not beneficial.

However, the characteristics of our spirit are hugely different. If we live out of our spirit, we will find that we are loving and prone to be gentle. We desire peace. We are considerate. We are far more contented when living out of our spirit. Also, joy will often have a great expression in our lives.

Sometimes, we have experienced traumas that create a situation of our soul not trusting our spirit. The soul blames the spirit for not protecting it. The irony is that, typically, our soul never gave place to the spirit so that it could protect us. The soul places false blame on the spirit, and it must be coerced to forgive the spirit. Then, the soul must relinquish control to the spirit. Once the soul forgives the spirit, the two components can begin to work in harmony.

If I were to flash an image of some delicious, freshly cooked donuts in front of us, what would happen? For many, their body would announce a craving for one. What if, instead, I showed an image of a bowl of broccoli? How many people would get excited about that? Probably not as much excitement over a bowl of broccoli would be exhibited. Which does our body prefer—the donuts or broccoli? For the untamed soul, the donuts are likely to win out every time. Which do most kids prefer?

In any case, we can train ourselves to go for the healthier option. A principle regarding this that I heard years ago is summed up like this:

*What we feed will live—
what we starve will die*

What do we want to be dominant—our spirit, our soul, or our body? The part we feed is the part that will dominate.

For some, they feed their soul and live by the logic of their mind. Everything must be reasoned out in their mind before they will accept it. However, because our soul gains its insight from the Tree of the Knowledge of Good and Evil, it will always have faulty and limited understandings.

How do we change this soul-dominant or body-dominant pattern? We instruct our soul to back up, and we call our spirit to come forward. Some people may need to physically stand up and speak to our soul and say, "Soul, back up," and as they say those words, take a physical step backward. Then, speak to their spirit out loud and say, "Spirit, come forward." As we speak those words, take a physical step forward. This prophetic act helps trigger a shift within them.

Live spirit first!

Benefits of Living Spirit First

Why would we want to live spirit first? Let me present several reasons. Living spirit first will create in us an increased awareness of Heaven and the realms of Heaven. It will create a deeper comprehension of the presence of Holy Spirit, of angels, and men and women in white linen. We will be able to better hear the voice of Heaven. We will experience greater creativity, productivity, hope, and peace. We will become more aware of the needs of people that we meet.

> *As we live spirit first,*
> *we will be able to access*
> *the riches of Heaven in our life.*

Petty things that formerly bothered us will dissipate in importance or impact in our lives. We will be able to move ahead, not concerned with the petty, mundane, or unproductive things that have affected our lives before we begin to live spirit first.

This way of life is more than a game changer—for the believer, it is the only way to live. We will face challenges as we build our business or live our lives from Heaven down, but we will more readily be able to access the solutions of Heaven as we live with an awareness of the richness of Heaven and all that is available to us as sons or daughters of the Lord Most High. Do not live dominated by the soul.

> *Live **spirit** first!*

∞

Resources from LifeSpring International Ministries

A visit to the **RonHorner.com** website will give a glimpse of the various branches of ministry we are involved in. We started by providing coaching to people within the Courts of Heaven, advocating for them and their situations. Our corporate name is LifeSpring International Ministries, Inc., a North Carolina registered nonprofit.

Personal Advocacy Sessions

Known as Personal Advocacy Sessions, these 90-minute sessions with our trained team of advocates have successfully worked with a myriad of situations. If you have an issue that you can't seem to get breakthrough about, schedule a session with our advocates.

LifeSpring Mentoring Group

Since starting this weekly class on Zoom in 2019, we have taught on the Courts of Heaven, protocols, engaging Heaven for revelation, working with angels and men and women in white linen, lingering human spirits, and more. It is a free class. Simply visit **ronhorner.com** to register for the link for the class.

Membership Program

We have several tiers of membership for those tracking with us. The Platinum level gains you access to our library of videos, blogs, and more. Again, visit the website.

LifeSpring School of Ministry

A trimester-based school to help you grow in your walk. Trimester 1 focuses on cleansing your generations. Trimester 2 focuses on Protocols of the Courts of Heaven, and Trimester 3 focuses on Advanced Protocols of the Courts of Heaven. Completion of Trimesters 1, 2, and 3 will qualify the student for consideration as a Junior or Senior Advocate able to conduct Personal Advocacy Sessions with our clients.

CoursNet

CourtsNet is our video-based training program offering a wide variety of classes and courses. We have free courses as well as paid courses.

AfterCare

Not every situation is solved by the Courts of Heaven. Sometimes people need to learn simple things to navigate life. Our AfterCare program provides Biblical counseling, classes, and groups regularly.

Sandhills Ecclesia

In 2022, we began a Sunday Gathering known as Sandhills Ecclesia, which is the name we saw on the book in Heaven when we went to inquire. My wife, Adina, and I live in the North Carolina area known as the Sandhills region, hence the name. We meet weekly at 11:00 AM Eastern Time, and on the first Sunday of each month, we have an afternoon gathering to conduct legislative work in the Courts of Heaven as a group. All are welcome. Simply visit **sandhillsecclesia.com** and register for the link.

Heaven Down Business

Heaven Down Business is a worldwide coaching and consultancy business designed to assist entrepreneurs and business owners in implementing the Heaven Down™ Business Building paradigm into their business. For more information, visit **heavendownbusiness.com**.

Adina's Melodies/Heaven Down Music

Adina Horner, co-founder, is a gifted minstrel and has several albums of prophetic worship music available on several of the most popular music platforms. Visit **adinasmelodies.com**.

LifeSpring Publishing/Scroll Publishers

LifeSpring Publishing primarily publishes Dr. Ron's books, and Scroll Publishers is our imprint where we publish the books of others relating to engaging Heaven, living spirit forward, and the Heaven Down™ lifestyle.

YouTube Channel

Our most recent videos from the Mentoring Group are posted on YouTube®. Visit our YouTube® channel,

Description

Embracing *Crowns for Your Business* is a clarion call to entrepreneurs, leaders, and visionaries who know their business is more than a career—it's a Kingdom assignment. Step into your royal identity and govern your business with divine strategy, spiritual authority, and Heaven's backing.

You weren't meant to build with earthly wisdom alone. You were crowned to partner with God, access heavenly blueprints, and steward resources that create lasting impact. Whether you're launching a startup, leading a team, or navigating marketplace challenges, this guide will help you align your business with God's purposes and flow in supernatural favor maximizing the crowns Heaven has for you.

Inside you'll discover how to:

- Discern the major assaults against your business.
- Intercede effectively for your business using the mantles Heaven has provided.

- Govern with integrity, authority, and prophetic insight.

Your business isn't just a vehicle for provision; it's a vessel for transformation. It's time to embrace your crown and lead with Heaven's perspective.

———— ∞ ————

About the Author

Dr. Ron Horner is an apostolic teacher specializing in the Courts of Heaven. He has written nearly forty books on the Courts of Heaven, engaging Heaven, working with angels, living from revelation, and most recently on Crowns of Authority.

He currently trains people in engaging the Courts of Heaven in a weekly online teaching session. You can register to participate and discover more about the Courts of Heaven prayer paradigm on his various websites, classes, products, and services found here:

www.ronhorner.com

———— ∞ ————

Other Books by Dr. Ron M. Horner

Building Your Business from Heaven Down

Building Your Business from Heaven Down 2.0

Building Your Business with the Blueprint of Heaven

Commissioning Angels – Volume 1

Cooperating with The Glory

Courts of Heaven Process Charts

Dealing with Trusts & Consequential Liens

Embracing Crowns for Governmental Intercession

Embracing Crowns for Your Business

Embracing Crowns for Your Family

Embracing Your Crown of Authority

Engaging Angels in the Realms of Heaven

Engaging Heaven for Revelation – Volume 1

Engaging Heaven for Revelation – Volume 2

Engaging Heaven for Trade

Engaging the Courts for Ownership & Order

Engaging the Courts for Your City (*Paperback, Leader's Guide & Workbook*)

Engaging the Courts of Healing & the Healing Garden

Engaging the Courts of Heaven

Engaging the Help Desk of the Courts of Heaven

Four Keys to Dismantling Accusations

Freedom from Mithraism

Kingdom Dynamics – Volume 1

Kingdom Dynamics – Volume 2

Let's Get it Right!

Lingering Human Spirits

Lingering Human Spirits – Volume 2

Living Spirit Forward

Maximizing Your Crown of Authority

Next Dimension Access to the Court of Supplications

Overcoming the False Verdicts of Freemasonry

Overcoming Verdicts from the Courts of Hell

Releasing Bonds from the Courts of Heaven

The Courts of Heaven: An Introduction
(formerly *Engaging the Mercy Court of Heaven*)

Unlocking Spiritual Seeing

Working with Your Realms and Your Realm Angels

SPANISH

Cómo Anular los Falsos Veredictos de la Masonería

Cómo Proceder en la Corte Celestial de Misericordia

Cómo Proceder en las Cortes para su Ciudad

Cómo Trabajar con Angeles en los Ambitos del Cielo

Cooperando con La Gloria de Dios

Las Cuatro Llaves para Anular las Acusaciones

Liberando Bonos en las Cortes Celestiales

Liberando Su Visión Espiritual

Sea Libre del Mitraísmo

Tablas de Proceso de la Cortes del Cielo

———— ∞ ————